CLOCK OUT AND HEAL

Gina Sanguinetti

ISBN 979-8-89130-282-2 (paperback)
ISBN 979-8-89130-283-9 (digital)

Christian Faith Publishing
832 Park Avenue
Meadville, PA 16335
www.christianfaithpublishing.com

Printed in the United States of America

Preface

Surprise, family. I said several times that one day I am going to finish journaling and maybe it will become a book. I recently returned to these unfinished writings and decided it was time to wrap it up. I then submitted a manuscript to this publisher but kept this a secret. I told absolutely no one about this new venture. But I must confess that Shannon overheard the phone call that I received from this publisher. I may be hard of hearing, but she is not, and I swore her to secrecy.

This is for you my children and grandchildren with all my love.

I thank God, my Savior, Jesus Christ, for life, family, and friends. I'm truly blessed.

Daughter Shannon and her husband, Robert
Daughter Stephanie and her husband, Steven
Daughter Brandi and her husband, Travis
Son Eric and his wife, Chelsea

My grandchildren, you are the stars in my eyes. I love you with all my heart and soul.

Olivia
Ryan and Maria
Jackson
Mia
Lucia
Nash
Grant
Brynley
Gia
Robert James (RJ)

> I can do all things through Him who strengthens me. (Philippians 4:13)

Chapter 1

Introduction

I began writing this book about twelve years ago. It started with a few short stories, mainly to journal about my experiences in my job. I needed an outlet, a way to face emotions, sadness, grief, stress, and sometimes frustrations. I work in the medical field as a respiratory therapist. You see, I was starting to realize that what we do as medical workers or those who are in service of all kinds really do have an effect on our bodies and mind. Medical personnel usually work twelve-hour shifts. We clock out, then go home and try not to think about the pain and suffering of those you served that day. We try not to think about the stress of our job, and we might put aside our own pain and emotions that occurred due to our workdays. I am grateful that I can help and serve people. I put in the extra effort to help patients, their families, and colleagues. Years go by, maybe even a couple of decades, and the emotions you hold back the trauma of seeing suffering, death, and heartache—start to surface in your mind in ways that are unexpected.

I suppressed heartache and grief after seeing and treating those who are suffering. I've seen countless and many types of death in all age groups. "It's part of the job" is what we say. We clock in, do what we are trained to do, clock out, go home, and forget about work. But you really don't forget, nice try though.

The job is not just seeing suffering and death, the job is demanding of more from each one of us. Much of the time during your shift, you feel as if you are swimming against the waves. Sometimes the waves turn into tsunamis. "Okay, I made it through this shift. It's time to clock out. I have just one more shift left for this week, then the week is over." This became the way I started to count time as weeks, months, and years swiftly passed.

As for me and most people I have observed in the medical field, any first responder field, and military, these jobs require strength and endurance to run a long haul in these services. If you are dedicated to give your best, have a stellar work ethic, go above and beyond the job description, the physical and emotional strength needed is not known until you are part of these worlds.

Once you decide that this is the job you want as a career, you accept the risks, the stress, the workload, the expectations from patients and their families, and the organization that employed you. You keep moving, going with the flow, accepting what is in the moment, and pushing through to get the job done again and again, day by day, year after year. You rejoice in the days that were easy, rejoice in the lives you helped heal, the lives you helped save, and how you made a difference today. But many of the days that were difficult, stressful, agonizing, and wearing were most likely put into a compartment in your heart and mind. Those emotions were meant to be dealt with when you had the time and energy to face it and deal with it. We dismissed, denied, declined to address much if not all of those stressful times. For me, I decided to write as my way of facing what I kept suppressed. But I found that each time I started to write, I would feel heartache reliving the pain that was incurred from my job. Therefore, I did not finish my journaling, my potential book. It was emotionally draining my energy to relive the trauma. I decided to put it all away where I don't have to face it. Basically, I decided not to think about it. I would tuck it away, make myself believe it was not there, and move along. After all, I am a strong person with faith. I didn't need to be concerned. I would be fine. I was believing I was fine. There was nothing I couldn't handle, until some of the denial started to manifest and surface. It showed up in some weird ways at different places and unexpected times.

One night, I was at a show in Atlantic City. There were crowds of people having fun, and I was having a great time with friends. I was walking among the crowds of people, enjoying the night, then suddenly a feeling of sadness overwhelmed me. I continued to walk through the crowds of people, and I began to feel that they were all sad as well. The sadness felt like the times during my workday when there was incidences of trauma or grief, such as in a code blue or a terminal extubation. What the heck just happened? I was having a fun night and now this sudden moment of sadness? *How dare you show up tonight when I am enjoying myself?* I was having a fun night and was not thinking about anything sad. After all, I buried those emotions, denied their existence, and continued to suppress them. I wasn't thinking about anything that was upsetting, so why would these emotions surface while I was having fun? I wasn't going to entertain or think about this rude interruption on my fun evening, so I once again shook it off and continued to have a good time, and I did have a fun night.

These occurrences would continue through the years, not often though. It never stifled or hindered my day; it was brief fleeing moments. I might have a few tears and felt some sadness, but I would then count my blessings, thank God for all He gives, then I was back to being myself again. Essentially, my life is a good one. I seek and have joy even through problems that may arise. God is my rock. He is the foundation that gives me hope, strength, and confidence of faith.

Recently I decided to finish my journaling, which I put aside for so long. I don't like to start something and then not finish it. Perhaps it's time to share with others in the medical field and other service jobs who have to clock out and put their emotions in a compartment too. I hope this book will help benefit you to let you know that some of us understand and to raise awareness of what we see and do. Your life and your service to others are valued and appreciated.

Chapter 2

An Overview of the Hospital World

There are no routine days when you work in a hospital. It doesn't matter what your job title is in the medical field; you learn to expect the unexpected. Respiratory therapists are first responders who also have scheduled patient care, as well as other tasks that are mandatory in this job. Our job is demanding, unpredictable, physically and emotionally challenging, as well as rewarding. This is my twenty-seventh year working as a respiratory therapist. I still love the rewards it brings because I help save lives, serve, and help heal people.

I interact with patients, their families, and many colleagues. Together, as a medical team, we communicate to each other so we may formulate treatment plans for our patients, as well as educate them and their caretakers. It is a constant twenty-four-hour practice for each patient experience while they are in the hospital setting. There are no quick fixes while treating illness or addressing emergencies; it requires teamwork, quick thinking in some instances, and quick actions. My desire is for everyone to be healthy and well, which does require effort and thought for every individual. Our bodies are unique and wonderfully made by God who loves us and desires for us to care for others as well as ourselves.

> For you formed my inward parts;
> You wove me in my mother's
> womb. I will give thanks to You
> for I am fearfully and wonder-
> fully made. (Psalm 139:13–14)

God's creations are unique, awe-inspiring, and amazing. The science that I learned in this practice has made me respect who God is more than ever. Life is made from life, anything living grows from a living organism. Life doesn't evolve from something that is a nonliving organism.

The health care system, or we can view it as the sick care system, changes with technology, pharmaceuticals, and regulations, to name just a few. This can become confusing to patients. And those of us who work in this field are forever learning by continuing education, as well as on the job training. Those of us who joined this profession so we can serve and help heal people see the many sides of this business. Yes, it is a business, and the expectations of the employers of this business adds to the stress put upon employees and the patients we treat as well. Rules and regulations dictate how we work. It can become frustrating and sometimes unsafe in this environment. Most medical personnel have your interest, care, and well-being foremost and prioritized in our work day. Please consider that we are working under circumstances that govern what we do, when we do it, how we do it. We are in it to win it for our patients. We want to practice the very best for you while we keep you safe and informed. Inside a hospital is a world that, unless you are working there, is difficult to understand.

Through the years, as I drive to work, my mind begins to hope for a good workday, a day that I will keep vigilant to serve and protect my patients, assist my colleagues, and give my best. I clock in, go to my locker to gather the tools I need, then listen to the report from the previous shift. My mind starts organizing and prioritizing scheduled treatments, mandatory tasks, charting, recording, scanning patient bracelets; it's all a part of the day. We are updated on rules and regulations; we receive reports that are sent via e-mails, given verbally, by signs on the walls, to name a few. The hospitals are viewed by security cameras. We press keypads or badge to get into doors and security areas. All this and more remind us of how we work while inside these walls. The environment is overstimulating from alarms, monitors, phones, voices, movement, interruptions, computers, and unexpected circumstances. There are never-ending noises, never-ending stimulation that affects the medical staff as well as our patients. During our shift, we want to give patients everything they need or what is requested from patients or families, plus all the things that mean the world to you. Many of us have been patients at one or more times ourselves, and we see and feel what you are experiencing in the hospital.

A typical respiratory staffing in a community hospital are three covering day shift and two covering night shift in a twenty-four hours. We cover the entire hospital and can be on every floor on any given day. Sometimes it feels like we are functioning in perpetual motion. Despite all the challenges medical personnel has to deal with, we are concerned about our patients. We understand how frightening it is to be a patient in a hospital setting. Not only are you sick and overwhelmed, the very environment of the hospital is stressful for you. We truly want to ease any anxieties, uncertainties, fears, and frustrations you may have.

When I look back at my personal experience, I am grateful that God gave me the strength and endurance to work this job because the job requires it. I'm grateful that I strived for good health and well-being by a healthy lifestyle because it is needed in this line of work. The physical and emotional demands are constant, so a healthy lifestyle of mind and body are germane to good performance.

Hospitals are a world in its own. Most people will not understand its functions unless you work in it. Take a peek through some of my experiences to understand what we see and do. I want to share some of my personal stories during my almost three decades of working this job. I hope it will bring some awareness of what we do and the need to support each other, whether you are the patient or the medical personnel. The following stories are real. These stories are from my experience, but names of the patients are changed to respect privacy.

Chapter 3

Sweet Angel Girl

I answered my hospital zone phone, and the feeling of dread began to stir up when I heard the words "we have a child being coded, ETA five minutes." As I sprint to the emergency department, I was quickly phoning my coworkers, who are respiratory therapists, to let them know about the call, knowing they would meet me there *stat*. The adrenaline began to increase as I arrived to the code room and quickly prepared to receive this child. Code calls are always accompanied by dreaded feelings, and knowing it is a child increases those feelings of dread. Administering CPR on anyone is not only sorrowful and somber, it is laborious, intense. But the worse scenario is CPR on a child because the prognosis is poor. The odds of resuscitation to return back to a quality status of life is poor.

Through the doors entered the paramedics. CPR was still in motion. Chest compressions and assisted breathing via Ambu bag were being administered for her as she lay motionless on the gurney. The paramedic continued CPR while giving report as this beautiful toddler was transferred from the gurney to our code bed. The paramedics carefully handed off the equipment in a smooth fashion so CPR was not interrupted. The verbal report by the paramedics stated that the child was sleeping and did not awaken. She was found by her parents not breathing and unconscious.

Our ER doctor and our pediatrician were present, and the code process continued. I double-checked the airway, made certain everything was in place and secure. When you are managing the airway, administering the breathing via Ambu bag with oxygen, you are standing directly by the patient's head. As I was breathing for her, I was constantly looking at her face. She was a beautiful toddler. She looked like a little angel. She lay motionless, as if in a sleep. I silently prayed that this would all be successful, that this child would not die.

Her parents were ushered into the room and sat by her. They were shocked with disbelief. One of our team members directed them to sit close to her and hold her hands. The physicians explained to the parents what we were doing and that we would do everything possible for their baby girl. Through tears and sobbing, the mom started to speak to her child while trying to brace herself while coping with this horror. She kept repeating to her baby that she and Daddy were here, telling her to wake up, that it would be okay and to open her eyes. I continued to focus on my job, but my heart was hurting as I heard her repeating pleas. I cannot imagine the terror these parents were feeling as they helplessly watched their child getting resuscitated and hoping she would not die.

Chest compressions and manual breathing continued without missing a beat. Chest compressions are vital for blood circulation, a part of what CPR is. It may not be known to a nonmedical worker that chest compressions are traumatic on the body. Resuscitation in itself is physically traumatic on a body, especially a child. I would glance at the parents as we continued our resuscitation efforts, their eyes firmly fixed on their child's face. It was heart-wrenching watching the parents and listening to their pleas that were filled with evoking sadness. The situation was extremely sad, but medical personnel must stay composed and concentrate on what they are trained to do. When you are in a situation such as this, a defense mechanism kicks in so that you can continue to perform your job but sort of remove the emotion. At least push it aside so it doesn't interfere with your work. It's somewhat like you are bodily there, doing what is needed to be done, yet part of you is removed to filter out the agony of it. It is difficult to explain this unless you have experienced it.

The code continued. The team worked in synchrony as we continued our attempts to resuscitate this child. Children should never have to go through this, but it does happen. Each moment that goes by that there is no heartbeat indicates that attempts are becoming futile, especially with a child. That sadness and anguish that we all were feeling kept thickening as we continued our efforts.

The doctor spoke again; his voice was calm and compassionate as he tried to control the silent tears now seen on his face. "We're doing everything possible," he would say at times to the parents as he continued running the resuscitation efforts. The doctor is also a father, but he conducted himself as a true professional while carrying out this daunting effort. The code recorder spoke and announced the amount of time that had now passed and what time the last medication was administered while breaths and chest compressions continued. As I breathed for her, I would look at her beautiful little face as she lay motionless. She reminded me of one of my granddaughters who was the same age. The feeling of dread began creeping up on me again, and I had to dismiss the emotion, continue what I was doing, stay composed and professional even though my heart ached.

The parents continued to talk to their baby through agonizing sobbing while still holding her hands, trying to keep themselves together. You can sense that they were losing hope but at the same time tightly holding on to any thread of hope. Time continued to pass. The team knew that nothing would probably change. There was no heartbeat, no breath, no movement from this precious child, no change on the monitor. We knew it would be soon that our dear doctors were going to start ceasing the efforts of resuscitation on her. The doctors would speak up again to inform the parents that we were doing everything possible. These physicians displayed compassionate leadership to everyone present while they expertly performed their job.

As we continued resuscitation, I do not recall the amount of time that passed, but it was longer than what we learned through the science that would indicate to cease efforts of CPR. We knew the attempts were looking to be futile because of the amount of time of CPR given and all other indicators that were shown. We were bracing ourselves as our physician began to inform the parents that we had been doing everything possible. He informed them that her heart was not beating. She was not breathing even though we tried everything. While pushing back his tears, our doctor calmly informed the parents that we were going to stop resuscitation efforts. There was no more we could do.

"We are so sorry. There is nothing more we can do. We are going to stop now." Our doctor choked back his grief. He was keeping his composure, yet the tears from his eyes revealed his grief.

The team then began to withdrawal our efforts of this resuscitation. It looked as if we were moving in slow motion as we stopped what we were doing; our efforts ceased—no more compressions, no assisted breathing, no more medications administered through the IV lines. She is gone.

My heart was hurting. We were all hurting for the death of this beautiful child. As I quietly removed my equipment, I slowly backed away so the parents could move closer to their child in their time of grief. Mom and Dad were mournfully weeping. They sobbed while speaking to their baby, saying how much they loved her, to please wake up.

Along with the team, I moved out of the area, my heart hurting. And with my eyes filled with tears, I looked back at them one more time. Mom and Dad were leaning over her, hugging their little girl so tightly, knowing this would be the last hugs they could give. Then Mom suddenly lifted her baby girl into her lap, cradling her and rocking her as she continued to weep. Dad stood up and encircled the both of them, the three of them together in one embracement. The sight and sounds of grief were so doleful, the heartbreaking final moments of parents holding their deceased child. You don't forget it.

My zone phone that I carry began ringing, I walked toward the doors to exit into the hallway while I answered the call. It was a call from a nurse, requesting for me to see another patient who needed a respiratory therapist. As I shook off my sadness, I gulped down some water and walked to the stairway in route to address this call. That's what we have to do, push the emotion away and continue the job.

In the following several months, the vision of Mom lifting up her deceased child and hugging her would randomly flash in my mind. This scene would be momentary, lasting only seconds, and the feelings of sadness accompanied it. Then it would all disappear. My comfort was knowing that this precious child was in beautiful heaven, being held by Jesus.

Chapter 4

Through the Glass Doors

The changing of shifts in a hospital setting consists of receiving and giving patient reports and can set a tone on how your day may go. It usually helps when you have coworkers that have a good attitude, a positive tone, and good camaraderie can make a difference on how your shift starts out. I was assigned to work in the ICU. At the time, we had eight ventilators running in our small community hospital.

As I arrived in the ICU, I looked around to see what nurses, doctors, aides, and other participators were on that shift. We work as a team, so it is important to familiarize yourself with other colleagues as soon as you enter your work assignment. We hope for uneventful days, knowing that there is no routine work when you are treating patients. Always expect the unexpected. You need that mindset or else the job can quickly drain or discourage you.

Due to the information I received in report, there was a patient that I was particularly interested in. She was intubated (breathing tube placed in her trachea) and on the ventilator. She had an emergent situation that required this route to be taken. There was no other way to save her life. The ICU had glass sliding doors for each individual room. You could see the patient's entire room through the glass, which also attributed to the patient's safety. I peered into her room but did not walk in at this time. The physician was at bedside, speaking to the patient named Mrs. Catherine, and there were many family members present at her bedside. Catherine was awake. She looked alert, no distress noted, no alarms sounding. Some of her family who surrounded her bed were holding her hands in a supportive and caring manner. I could not hear the conversations due to the glass doors that were closed at this time, but I noted she would write something on paper and show the physician and family. The report I received this morning was that Catherine had inoperable cancer in her throat that became swollen and cutting off her ability to breathe. The breathing tube was inserted to keep her airway open, and then she was put on the ventilator to assist breathing. The cancer was inoperable, prognosis was grim, and it was reported that Catherine was aware of this futile prognosis and options.

The physician exited Catherine's room and approached me and the nurse taking care of

Catherine. I could see by the look on his face that he seemed uncomfortable. He began to tell us the plan and that he would be writing orders momentarily, which included me and the team that were participating in her care. The plan consisted of Mrs. Catherine's request to discontinue the breathing tube and ventilator. She and her family were aware and clearly informed that her throat was obstructed due to the cancer, but Catherine chose not to die on a ventilator. No medical treatments were going to change the inevitable; the cancer would cause her to die. The doctor stated when the nurses were ready that I was to remove her breathing tube. Her throat would probably close again, but he was not sure how long it would be until this unfortunate demise would take place. He showed compassion for Catherine and expressed his compassion for us as well since we were the team taking care of her and were implementing the physician orders as well as patient's requests.

"Catherine does not want any pain medicine or sedation. She wants to remain awake while her family surrounds her," he said with sympathy in his voice. "She is wide awake, aware, and appropriate. And the family confirmed that they knew of her requests as well and would be supportive. It may be upsetting as we wait and see how this will unfold."

That dreaded feeling arose in my gut once again, so I shook off that feeling because we had a job to do. The nurse approached me about a half hour later, stating that Catherine and her family were ready for us to extubate (take out breathing tube). The nurse had medication that was ordered in her hand in case Catherine changed her mind and decided to allow this medication to help her through the pain and suffering.

Together, the nurse and I entered the room and introduced ourselves. The family seemed supportive and comforting as they sat close to her bed; Catherine's hands were lovingly held by them. The room was quiet and solemn. The window blinds were opened as daylight permeated the room. It was a clear day, and Catherine welcomed the sunshine. Catherine looked up, nodded, and smiled at us, though the breathing tube hindered some of her facial movements. It appeared that she truly was comfortable with what was to unfold, and she was going to be strong for her family. I thought to myself that she was quite a strong-willed woman, and that is how she appeared to us that morning. The family stated they were ready, and Catherine nodded in agreement. We invited the family to remain in the room while we removed the ventilator and tube if they choose to observe the extubation. They could exit the room if they choose to do so. Either way, the choice is respected and supported by the staff. We support our patients' families and loved ones on whatever decision they choose. The patients' wishes are first and foremost.

Catherine began writing on the paper that was attached to the clipboard and motioned for all of us to read it. She wrote that she was ready and wanted to begin. She reminded us that she wanted to stay awake and for death to be a natural process. I can feel that sinking feeling in my heart. I can't imagine this kind of request for myself, but her family was honoring and supporting her requests. She made her wishes known prior to her grim cancer diagnosis and did not change her mind. Some of the family decided they would step out of the room but remain nearby. They would return to Catherine's side as soon as the breathing tube was removed. Most of the family that remained at bedside were calm, quiet, and supportive for this dear lady. We explained the procedure to Catherine, and her facial expression did not change. She had a confident and determined affect. Her eye contact was consistent as she looked at everyone in the room. She was engaging to all that were present and still indicated that she was fine with this decision. This was her well-thought-out plan, her final request, her last show of dignity.

We quietly and thoroughly set up a few pieces of equipment and were ready to remove the breathing tube. I explained each step as I performed them. She would nod throughout each sentence or question I asked. She tolerated the short procedure well, and the breathing tube was gently and successfully removed without incidence. Her eyes were fixed on mine as I gathered the tube and remnants of the extubation. I cleaned up her face, inserted an oxygen cannula in her nostrils, made certain everything was in place so the oxygen tubing fit comfortably under her chin. She remained calm while still smiling, and I would like to add that she showed courage and strength. We quickly removed the ventilator and any extra equipment to clear space so the family could have more room at her bedside. The family who had exited the room and were standing by the door were motioned to enter and told that everything went well. They quietly entered the room and took their seats to once again surround Catherine. They gently spoke to her and continued to show their loving support and gentle manner to her. Even though the breathing tube was removed, Catherine could not speak due to her obstructed cancerous throat. This lovely woman continued to smile. Her eyes were bright and alert. She had the attention of everyone present. I noticed her expression never changed, and her family's expression remained the same. You can see that the family was solemn. But at the same time, their responses to Catherine were accommodating and supportive. The family was carrying out this dear lady's last request that her death would be natural, and the tone around her would be that of contentment and peace. My tasks were now complete, and I was about to exit the room and continue my workday. I leaned over to talk near Catherine's ear, letting her know that we were nearby to attend to her needs and not to hesitate to ask for anything. She nodded twice, her eyes still focused on my eyes, her smile never leaving her dear face.

I then exited her room. It was time to catch up with my work. There were seven more patients with ventilators to check into. As I went from room to room, attending to other patients, I would glance over at Catherine's room. She was still awake with her family surrounding her. The scene did not change at all, as if it was snapped shot. The nurse would let me know if anything new was happening. She kept me informed as often as possible.

The nurse said, "I check on her often. She is not in distress but maybe a bit uncomfortable, but she still does not want medication."

I thanked the nurse. She was observant and took great care of her patients.

Several hours passed by, and essentially everything in Catherine's room was the same. But then a change came. I was in another room with a patient when the nurse entered and informed me that Catherine was showing signs of increased work of breathing and moderate distress. She stated that the family expressed their concerns about this, but Catherine was still declining any medication when offered to her. The nurse and I walked into Mrs. Catherine's room. The family looked up at us. The look of concern and even some of fright were noted on all their faces, but not with Catherine. Although she was moderately struggling, looked noticeably uncomfortable, the look of determination and confidence remained on her face. *My goodness*, I thought, *she is an incredibly strong-willed woman.* Most people would request medication if they were in this circumstance. The nurse informed her that we had the prescribed medication at hand if she would like to have it. It might be a good idea to use the medication to help her be more comfortable. In a gentle manner, her family was gently suggesting for her to use the medicine, also stating that it would help her to be more comfortable. Catherine looked at her family then looked at me. I nodded at her. She thought for a moment, and then she pinched her thumb and forefinger to show us that she agreed to a little bit and nodded yes. The family seemed relieved. They stated to this dear lady that she made a good decision. The nurse administered the medicine, and it helped with taking the edge off the distress that she had. The scenario remained peaceful and calm, and both the family and the patient appeared more restful.

More time passed, and still the scene in the room did not change. Her family remained at her bedside, calmly speaking to Catherine, showing her love, support, and respecting her dignity. The nurse informed me that Catherine decided to take a little more medication, and she was not struggling as much. In fact she began to close her eyes at times, as if she was taking catnaps, and looked less laborious. The room still remained quiet, the family never leaving Catherine's bedside. Nearing the end of my shift, Catherine peacefully and with dignity succumbed to her death. Her family remained by her side for a few more hours and said their last good-byes. As the family exited her room, they expressed their gratitude to the staff. They were thankful for the way we treated Catherine and everyone present with her. We respect the time and requests that the patients' loved ones have so they can grieve the way they choose and spend their time with their loved ones in their last moments.

Chapter 5

Birth–Death: What Is the Story in That Dash?

We see it on gravestones, date of birth, a dash (–), then the date of death. What did that dash represent for each life? How are they remembered, and what was their legacy? Was their time on earth a happy one? Were they sick? How did they die? Were there any family and friends? Headstones on graves only show dates and few, if any, other information. Some of the graves were that of babies' and children's; their lives were so short. What was the story of the brief time that a baby or child lived? How do we also represent a baby that was deceased prior to their birth or who died right after being born?

In the hospital setting, I witnessed many and different types of births. For the most part, a birth is an immediate and joyous occasion for the parents and their families. I still remain fascinated when I witness a birth; it is a miracle of life to see a baby born and to thrive. A baby born is usually a unique celebration of a new and precious life. Respiratory therapists have to respond to any birth that may have a possible complication, such as a meconium that can lead to a dangerous aspiration or a mother who has drug or alcohol addiction. If a distress of a baby is seen on a fetal monitor while birth is in process, we are also called to standby in the birthing room. We are called in case we are needed to assist in a resuscitation of the baby. We may have to implement and to use equipment in assisting a distress situation of a newborn. Expect the unexpected—we have seen many unexpected and frightening scenarios when babies are born. You have to be ready in all situations. I dread getting those calls that involve a baby who is going to be born "anytime now," but we arrive to wait and see for what may be. We are involved in all scenarios while a mother is birthing her baby, sometimes arriving just minutes after the baby unexpectedly arrived. In some cases, the babies that were born needed no help from us, but we were there because we were called just in case. There were babies born that were distressed, who needed short-term intervention, perhaps a little help to breathe from a CPAP machine, which usually resulted in a good outcome for the newborn. And we always rejoiced and felt relieved by good outcomes. We had calls when there was no heartbeat from the newborn after the birth and had to resuscitate and ventilate those neonates. Those cases were the worst-case scenarios and usually resulted in poor prognosis, and we grieved in those situations.

There are cases of mothers that gave birth, knowing their baby may be deceased. We saw miscarriages, also births of very premature infants that could not survive. Every case that involved sick babies is heartbreaking. Babies are vulnerable and fragile. You want the start of their life to a have a healthy beginning, and unfortunately, some have traumatic beginnings; some have tragic demise. I was fortunate to work by the side of some talented neonatologists in the community hospital that I worked in. We appreciated their respect for the life of a baby and to treat every one of those precious neonates in a unique and caring way. The neonatologists would give every effort possible while those babies were our patients. Most of the very sick babies had to be transported to a specialty hospital. There were babies that didn't need to be transported, and they remained in our NICU while they healed, and most of them thrived.

The number of tubes sometimes needed and inserted into their little bodies would look overwhelming. Special precautions were taken by all staff while handling these neonates. After all, babies are so small and fragile, a premature baby even smaller than a baby of full-term. Some of these neonates required breathing tubes inserted into their airways and to be put on ventilators. What we do to treat sick babies still amazes me;

I consider it miraculous. Babies are helpless and vulnerable. It is part of the job that you are more vigilant when you treat them. We are their voice as well as their caretakers while they are in our care. Babies are totally dependent on us.

My heart hurts for those sick little humans. My heart hurts also for their moms, dads, and their families. When you are treating sick babies, you can see and hear the sadness coming from the parents as they helplessly watch the medical team attend to their children's needs. They feel helpless and are depending on you to care for their babies as they clutch onto any hope for signs that their babies are going to be okay.

I want to acknowledge all the precious little humans we saw that never breathed, that never had a heartbeat. I acknowledge those precious little humans that had a very brief life; their heart stopped soon after birth, and we could not bring them back. I acknowledge babies that had a short life, died when they were young, and had only a brief time on earth. I want to acknowledge the mothers who gave birth and grieved because it was a stillbirth, a mother who grieved due to a premature birth that could not be saved, a grieving mom who had a miscarriage, a mother who grieved due to an abortion. To all the dads and the families who grieved, your babies were all special and precious in the eyes of God. He created each one unique and wonderfully made. My comfort is to know that each one of those deceased babies are with God.

They are valued and precious in His heaven. I pray for your comfort and leave you with God's words, some reference from the Bible.

> Before I formed you in the womb I knew you, before you were born I set you apart. (Jeremiah 1:5)

> Children are a gift from the Lord. They are a reward from Him. (Psalm 127:3)

> See that you do not despise one of these little ones, for I say to you that their angels in heaven continually see the face of my Father who is in heaven. (Matthew 18:10)

> So it is not the will of your Father who is in heaven that one of these little ones perish. (Matthew 18:14)

> Behold, children are a gift of the Lord, the fruit of the womb is a reward. (Psalm 127:3)

Chapter 6

Mrs. Rose

In the middle of the patient report, the beginning of the shift, a stat request received was to assess a patient named Mrs. Rose. I hurried to the floor and into her room where the nurse was present at the bedside. As I approached the patient, she seemed to be somewhat lethargic, had mild distress even though she still greeted me with a frail and weak smile. The nurse reported she was moving about in her bed, trying to get onto the commode, and became mildly short of breath, but vitals were now stable. I started to assess Mrs. Rose, and the nurse left the room to get her chart and to call the physician. Though she looked exhausted, Mrs. Rose was able to speak to me without difficulty; she was aware and appropriate. I helped her get comfortable in bed. She wished to sit up, so I helped to position her until she felt comfortable. I asked her some brief questions. And though she was fatigued, she pleasantly answered, and I continued with my assessment. Mrs. Rose was a woman who apparently cared about her appearance. I noticed that her hair was neatly brushed. Her face looked washed. There was a basin of water with soaps, and lotions were on her table at arm's reach. She was also wearing lipstick. Her appearance was neat and clean. She had pretty eyes that looked soft and clear. There was a twinkling in them as she began to brighten up and was gaining some energy. Her room was quiet and orderly; everything in her surroundings seemed to be in place. There were delightful floral scents coming from fresh flower arrangements, which seemed to be strategically placed in her room.

I finished my assessment and informed her that I was going to speak to her nurse, who would return to see her shortly. She nodded her head, still smiling. She then said to me that she was thirsty and would like to have some juice. I told her I would be glad to get her juice. I wanted to speak to her nurse first to make sure that it was okay for me to give it to her.

"What kind of juice would you like? We have apple, grape…"

She didn't hesitate to say "grape, please. I'm so thirsty, and I love grape juice."

She continued to smile, and I let her know I would shortly return and asked her to call for assistance if she needed to use the commode again. "We don't want you to fall, so please let us help you."

She nodded in agreement, the smile never changed.

I located her nurse to make sure Mrs. Rose was permitted to have juice. I don't know her dietary orders and if there were restrictions, so it was a must to ask before giving her anything to drink or eat. The nurse said it was okay to give her the juice, and I also inquired about her medical condition and other information that I needed before I documented my notes. The nurse informed me that she was a DNR and DNI (do not resuscitate; do not intubate). She also informed me that Mrs. Rose was doing poorly, that she was failing. The nurse said she had spoken with her daughter this morning, and her daughter was getting ready to drive to the hospital; it was more than an hour drive. The nurse also informed me that Mrs. Rose requested for her daughter to get to the hospital, that she wanted to see her as soon as possible. The nurse told me that she did not have a good feeling. She looked forward for the arrival of Mrs. Rose's daughter and knew that she would be comforting for Mrs. Rose.

I went to the pantry and grabbed some grape juice, filled a cup with ice, and returned to the room. The nurse was once again assisting Mrs. Rose, who was now sitting on the commode. I told the nurse I could stay with her and that I would help her back into bed and help her drink the grape juice. Mrs. Rose stated she was ready to get back into bed, so I was poised to assist her and to make sure to keep her from a possible fall. While I was assisting her to get back into bed, she suddenly had a burst of energy and pretty much hopped into her bed without much help from me. It was if she was taking a leap from the commode into her bed. I was surprised that she had such a burst of energy, and she did not have shortness of breath or distress. There was a vast improvement in her compared to when I first walked in. I helped her get comfortable and then adjusted the height of her bed so she was sitting upright to drink her juice.

"Well, ma'am, here is your grape juice. I can help you if you would like."

She took the cup from my hand and drank it down so quickly, even after I cautioned her to drink a little slower. I didn't want her to aspirate the juice.

"Oh, my goodness, this is good. I'm so thirsty," she said as she looked at me. Her eyes twinkled. She continued to smile. She drank all of the juice and commented how good it tasted. She seemed content and satisfied. I thought to myself that she looked better than earlier. And when I asked her how she was now feeling, she replied that she felt good, that she was okay.

"My daughter is on her way to visit me." She seemed so happy and comforted speaking those words. I said that I was glad her daughter was on her way to see her.

"Is there anything more I can do for you?" I asked.

"No, I'm fine," she spoke as she kept smiling. She seemed happier and stronger. I told her I would stop by later to check on her again. I could see that she did not take her eyes off me, nor did she stop smiling as I was exiting her room. *What a lovely woman,* I thought. I continued on to resume my work. I was behind and needed to catch up with the scheduled work on my list. So I continued in and out of rooms, patient after patient, trying to catch up on what I needed to do. I needed to drink some water and grab something to eat. I decided to take a break soon after I caught up with my workload.

After I completed my tasks, I headed to the cafeteria, then the phone rang. It was the nurse who took care of Mrs. Rose. She sounded solemn and sad.

"Mrs. Rose died soon after you left her room. When I went in to check on her, she looked as if she was sleeping. But when I tried to awaken her, she did not respond. She was gone. Sadly, her daughter did not arrive in time."

I decided to go back to Mrs. Rose's room. The nurse was still present at her bedside. I took Mrs. Rose's hand and whispered that I was glad to have met her. I won't forget her twinkling eyes. I turned to the nurse and said, "Maybe just knowing that her daughter was on the way to see her was all she wanted to hear."

Chapter 7

My Best Friend's Dad

I was at the nurses' station, documenting my work, when I heard a familiar voice. I looked over to see that it was my best friend's mom, and I also affectionately refer to her as Mom. It was a surprise to see her, and I walked over to her and said hi.

"Whatcha doing here?"

She told me her husband, my best friend's dad, was here and was a patient on this floor. She continued to explain what was going on, that he was having some shortness of breath at this time. Of course she was concerned and asked if someone could see him. I immediately went to his room, and while entering, it took just seconds to see that he had mild laborious breathing. He was not in distress but definitely needed some attention. Perhaps a call to the physician and some breathing treatments might help him. As I approached his bed, he immediately noticed who I was, and he smiled at me. He was able to speak in short sentences and said he was having some trouble catching his breath. It was not an emergency, but he needed my attention, so I did an assessment on him then reported to the nurse and physician. I informed Mom and Pop that I received the doctor's order to administer treatments and stayed with them while he took his nebulizers. Mom took a seat by his bedside. The room was quiet until I spoke to explain what the doctor ordered and to inform them with other information.

I was familiar with his medical history; lung disease was a part of it. I was young when I first met my best friend and her family. We may have been about six years of age, living only a few short blocks from each other in a small town on the seashore. He and his wife were married for more than a half century, and they had five children. In his younger years, he was a strong, hardworking man. He made a living in sales and other jobs until retirement. He was also a veteran and a respected citizen in our community.

In the later years, as he aged, he started to get sick due to disease of the lungs. I knew he prepared himself for the progression and prognosis of his disease. He was that type of person to be realistic and to make plans. He would fight the disease, and when the time came, he accepted what was to be the end with dignity and strength. He organized his affairs. His end-of-life requests were made known to his family who respected and carried out his wishes.

While Pop finished his treatments, I continued to observe him and talk with the both of them. After he finished his breathing treatments, I assessed him again. The treatments helped out a little, considering he had advanced disease. But more importantly he appeared to look calmer, less labored. He answered my questions with short sentences. His voice was weak, and his body was fragile. Both the state of disease progression and age weathered him physically. He was now frail and weakened. This man, who had a strong commanding voice, now spoke with a voice that was soft, weak, and strained. It saddened me to think how the role was now reversed. The man who once took care of and provided for his family was now in need of care. I know this is life, but it still hurts the heart.

"Did that breathing treatment help you?" I asked him.

He nodded and said yes. He looked more comfortable, and I know Mom felt relieved that he felt improved. He then picked up a breathing therapy device that was lying on the table near him and began using it. He seemed to find comfort with this therapy, which was okay with me. He said the therapy helped him breathe easier.

Soon I had to go and wrap up my last rounds. It was nearing the time to clock out and go home. I could feel my eyes starting to tear up as I choked back a sob that was starting to creep up on me. It was difficult for me to tell him I needed to leave and finish my work. I repeated to them that "we are here to help, so please don't hesitate to ask." I knew them well, and they were the type of people that did not request much help from others. I said I would return later after I clock out this evening at the end of my shift. I nodded to the both of them and exited the room to continue my work. There was little time left until my shift ended. I was still feeling sad, but I had to shake it off for now and keep moving along.

It was the end of my shift, and I clocked out, wrapping up another day. But I wanted to check in on Pop, my best friend's dad. I knew, by this time, his wife went home because visiting hours were over, and she had to drive a distance. I gently knocked on his door and announced I was coming in, if it was okay. He signaled to come in, so I approached his bedside. He was sitting up halfway in the bed. He appeared comfortable, no distress noted. With his frail, soft voice, he slowly spoke in short sentences, which was all he was able to do.

"Hi," I said, "I wanted to check in on you before I go home. What can I do for you? What do you need?"

He looked right at me, his eyes to my eyes. A few seconds past, as if he was thinking prior to speaking. I kept eye contact with him, and then he spoke. "I don't need anything, but I want to say thank you for everything."

It was the way he said this statement as well as what he said that gripped me, and I could feel the tears forming in my eyes. I felt the gut feeling that I experienced too many times, that feeling of finality. I hate it. I hate those moments. I knew this was the last time I was going to see him. He knew it as well. We continued to look at each other. He knew what I was thinking. The moment was so silent, but it seemed so loud. His thank-you was his way of showing me care and concern at this time that I was showing care to him. I leaned over and gave him a hug. He was so fragile and weak.

"I wish I can make you better," I said. My voice was cracking, I was trying not to cry.

His eyes stayed fixed on mine. He was looking at me as if to comfort me, as if he was telling me that he was okay. Then he said, "Thank you for what you do."

I could feel the sobs that were starting to emerge in me. I didn't want to cry. I then straightened myself into a standing position, poised to get ready to leave. I smiled an awkward smile, fighting back tears that were now dampening my face. "I'll see you again on my next shift," my voice was rasping. "The night shift will be stopping in to see you soon. Let them know when you need anything." I slowly backed out of the room. We still looked at each other, both of us trying to give a comforting smile. His smile might be frail, but it was just for me, and I will treasure it always. I still see it as I recall this moment. As I moved toward the door, it was difficult for me to turn away, knowing this might be our last goodbye. It was our last goodbye.

Chapter 8

We're Born, We Live, We Die—Then What?

From the time I was young, I grew up learning a religion that never felt right to me. It was ritualistic and required practices that seemed strange, but my parents enforced it at an early age and into my teenage years. I knew in my heart that God existed, but I did not buy the spin-off of the religion that we were part of. As I entered my preteen years, I started to question as to why we were following this religion. I stated that God is everywhere. Why did I have to practice certain rituals that seemed to revolve around religion that was formulated by man rather than just believe the Bible? At a young age, I believed at that time that the Bible is God's words, and I believe it more so now. I was taught in this religion to pray ritual and repetitive prayers, but I also talked with God in my own words, knowing in my heart that He heard me. It was important for me that God would hear my words in the way that I spoke them. I also began questioning why parts of life could be unfair, why people would die even though it was at an old age, that what I saw and all I knew as I grew up was that only older people die. I clearly recalled when my paternal grandfather died when I was about eight years of age.

It was a lovely summer day, and all of us were outside, playing in the swimming pool. My grand-pop was sitting in his usual chair in his usual spot in the shade. He would relax and enjoy the fresh air as his grandchildren played nearby. Then there was a day that he looked like he was napping. He quietly drifted away and died that afternoon, right in his chair. Years prior to that, when I was about three years old, his wife, my paternal grandmom, was very ill. I remember her crying and speaking Italian while she was sitting up in her bed at home. She was wearing an oxygen mask, and there was a large oxygen tank at her bedside. My dad was hold-ing me, so grandmom could see me through that large scary-looking oxygen mask. He instructed me to talk to Grandmom and that she was very sick, and it would make her feel happy that I was visiting her. It is a little difficult for a child to see those sce-narios. It was a bit frightening to me because I was very young and didn't understand why Grandmom looked so sick and that she was crying. Even though I was very young, I somehow knew that it would be okay, and this is what we had to do for Grandmom.

Through the years I attended funerals, viewings, and funeral church services because of deaths that occurred in my large Italian-descent family. I started to realize that this is part of life. The elderly would die; you respected what happens and accept it as part of life. In those times of having to attend funerals, there was at least one outlet of comfort; I was going to see all my cousins during the services. My cousins and I would group together, as kids usually do, and have a little fun playing, just like kids should do. After the services were over, there was always a luncheon at a venue, and we kids would continue to play and have fun together. After the luncheon was over, we would then go to the home that was nearby to one of our relatives. Care and catering revolved around the surviving elderly person who was now the focus due to the death of their spouse. Neighbors and friends visited their home to bring more food and show respect to the family. The care and love of people visiting eased those times of grief, and you looked forward to seeing those people. I never saw those times as traumatic or stressful. They were times of togetherness with loved ones and friends. As a kid growing up, you just knew that this is part of life; this is how it works. One day you will grow old and either die in your sleep or become ill and then die. It wasn't until middle-school years that I had my first experience that older people were not the only ones that died.

Living in a small town, we grew up with the community kids and attended school with them as well. School was a lot of fun because kids essentially got along well, and life seemed easier and more relaxed in those days. There were activities during school, during recess, after school, and on weekends, and we were always active and had lots of fun. A camaraderie among the town's children was normal. It was a way of life for us. They were your schoolmates as well as your friends.

One day, there was tragic news about one of our classmates, our friend, a boy my age. The news swept through our small town, and we could not believe it was true. Our dear friend was hit by a car and was gone; the news was surreal. My friends and I gathered and spoke about this tragedy. But it couldn't be true. After all, children do not die. Who could ever experience such a thing?

As a group, we decided we should bake a cake and bring it to the family of our young deceased friend. We baked the cake. And once again, as a group, we walked it over to his home and presented it to his family. It was our way of showing our care, though we were still in disbelief that this happened. A few days later, we would be meeting outside the funeral home so we could walk into the building once again as a group. We knew that there would be a viewing of our friend, so we chose to walk in together. It seemed easier and more comforting that way.

After the viewing of our dear friend, we sat in the chairs that were positioned in front of the coffin that held our friend. It was time for the priest to perform his services. We sat and were attentive, quiet, and respectful. I don't remember everything he spoke about, but I do remember the words *heaven* and *God*, and it sparked something in me. My mind opened, and I started to think, if there was a heaven, how do we get there if it truly existed? At this stage in my young teenage years, I wanted to know if there is a heaven. If there is a heaven, I don't want to miss out on going there. After all, it sounded like an awesome, outstanding place. That very moment, I silently asked God to show me answers, to let me learn if there was an existence of heaven and hell. I learned a little bit about it in religion class and in church but was not sure if there were choices to be made or if God just appointed certain people to be ascended or descended into those places. The religious explanations of heaven and hell were explained in simple but not plausible terms, so I had doubts of their existence. In my own young mind, I needed to know more about these so-called eternal places, if these places truly existed, and if we have choices in all this. I wanted answers but did not know how to find those answers. But somehow, I knew that God was going to let me know. In hindsight, I now realize that this was the day my mind and heart were opened, and I knew that God would provide this information for me, but I did not know how he was going to do that. It wasn't until a few years later that I started to receive answers to those questions that I had given to God. In my senior year of high school, we lost two more friends from tragic death. Once again, I questioned God because I wanted to know why and how all this works. I did not want to miss out on a good thing if that good thing was available for me and my loved ones.

In the later part of the 1970s, the answers to my questions were starting to be revealed to me. There were family members that talked about Jesus that had never talked about that subject until now. There was a pastor that became acquainted with my extended family and then became a family friend to us. Proof was shown to me by the words in the Bible, and I also saw positive changes in the lives of some of my family and other extended family. In my heart, I finally began to realize the truth. It was becoming clear to me that I now have the answer to those questions. The answer was not complicated. It was shown to me in the Bible, and I began to believe it. My eyes were opened. The truth set me free. A feeling of relief accompanied my revelation. I now knew my eternity was sealed. I had a hope and peace that I didn't know before. My heart accepted Jesus as my Savior, and I believed this in my mind as well. For the rest of my earthly life, I am now sealed with an "assurance policy" that I still hold true throughout my years. Actually, my faith and relationship with Jesus have grown in the past several years, and my life is experiencing more peace and joy as a result of growing faith. I want everyone to know that there are answers. We're born. We live, and there are choices to be made that are life-changing, choices to be made here and now. We're born. We live. We die. And then there is an eternity. The choice is to be made while we live.

I'm grateful that I accepted the answer that was shown to me. I had no doubts when I was a teenager and gave my heart to Jesus. I know that God loves all of us. He created us in His image, and we are unique and wonderfully made. God desires relationship with us. It is an individual choice, a choice I made. No matter who we are, what we've done, where we are now, His grace is free to all of us. Jesus gave His life for all, and whoever accepts Him as Savior will have eternal life with him. He just wants our hearts. He asks that we ask for forgiveness from our wrongdoings, our sins, and that we acknowledge that He died for us. It is an individual choice, and I pray for everyone to make that choice now.

Here are a few verses from the Bible about salvation:

> For God so loved the world, that
> He gave His only son, whoever
> believes in Him will not perish
> but have eternal life. (John 3:16)

> And they were saying to the
> woman, "It is no longer because
> of what you said that we believe,
> for we have heard for ourselves
> and know that this one is indeed

the savior of the world." (John 4:42)

If you confess with your mouth Jesus is Lord and believe in your heart that God raised Him from the dead, you will be saved. (Romans 10:9)

Looking for the blessed hope and the appearing of the glory of our great God and Savior Christ Jesus, who gave himself for us to redeem us from every lawless deed, and to purify for Himself a people for His own possession, zealous for good deeds. (Titus 2:13–14)

My God, my rock, in whom I take refuge, my shield and the horn of my salvation, my stronghold and refuge, my savior. (2 Samuel 22:3)

Chapter 9

Till Death Do We Part?

I loved you. You loved me. I still love you. Time and circumstances parted us. We said that love wasn't enough to keep it together and went our separate ways. Sadly, time and circumstances were beyond control. The timing continued to be off, especially when stress clouded our thinking and decision-making.

I will never forget the day I received the phone call from you. It was while I was at work at the hospital. You told me you had bad news. Those words pierced my heart, and that feeling of dread began to surface in me. I tightly held on to the phone, and I asked you to hold on while I searched for a quiet place so you could tell me why you were calling. I nervously walked the hospital hallways and found a quiet area on another floor. I was ready to hear the bad news. In a calm and steady voice, you informed me that you had inoperable lung cancer, and you made an appointment with an oncologist in the hospital I work in. I couldn't believe this news. My heart sank, and a sick feeling gripped me, I was starting to cry. I couldn't hold it in, and you told me it would all be okay. You told me that you wanted to tell the kids. My kids were your family from the beginning, and it was so appreciated that you were the father figure in their lives. You were their step-dad, a part of the family, and they haven't and will not forget you.

You told me the date of your oncology appointment; it was a long time away. So I offered to speak with the oncologist to see if it was possible to make the appointment sooner. I wanted to have more time to cry, and I wanted to go home and deal with what you just told me. I had to pull myself together, and I made a call to the oncologist. It was a relief to hear that she was able to fit you in for an earlier appointment. When I called you and gave you the new appointment date, you were glad to hear it. You wanted to start any treatment that was recommended to you.

In these upcoming days, we sometimes talked about us. Even though we both were in a different place in our own lives, our connection remained. You went through chemo treatments. You wore a brave face through all of it. You knew your prognosis was poor, and you prepared for the end of your life and accepted it with dignity and strength. Everyone noticed a joy and peace in you as you continued to enjoy your remaining days. You were determined that you would enjoy your time with family, making the best of each day, until there were no more days. Being the organized person that you were, you set up your wishes, made the preparations that satisfied who you were. The remaining time you had was thoughtfully spent with your family and friends.

As you lived your last days, you decided to have peace with God and accepted who He is. At times we talked. We spoke of our time together, the good times we cherished. We had times that we reminisced, shared some regrets, and made peace with each other. More than ever, I cherish those times we spoke of, though we were not together. A bond still remained.

The phone call I received that you were in the hospital and it did not look good shook me. I knew this would be the last time I would see you as I arrived at the hospital. You were asleep due to sedation and on a ventilator, waiting to be transported to another hospital. I stood at your bedside. I hated that a ventilator had to breathe for you. You were sedated and asleep. I wanted to see you awake one more time but knew I wouldn't. I leaned over and spoke in your ear, hoping you heard me. One more I love you was whispered to you, and my heart hurt terribly. This was it, one more time and the last time we would part our ways. This time would be the final time on earth.

You were transported to another hospital, but the attempts to save your life were futile. You were made comfortable, taken off life support while surrounded by your family until you succumbed to death. I knew when the phone rang that it would be the news that you were gone. We still miss you. I miss you. I think of you. I sometimes look up into the stars and talk to you. "Miss you. Love you. See you soon."

Chapter 10

You Are the Salt of the Earth, the Elderly

Starting from a young age, my childhood, I liked elderly folks, and I still like elderly folks. In my younger years, I wasn't sure what fascinated me about elderly people; I just knew I liked being around them. The elderly usually had stories to tell, which I found those stories interesting and sometimes entertaining. It seemed to me that elderly folks usually seemed content, essentially happy, and peaceful, at least that was what I saw in my surroundings. My experience with the elderly when I was a kid were folks that were retired. They spent their time gardening, cooking, reading newspapers, and they liked young folks to talk with. I found their lifetime of experience fascinating, and I absorbed their stories and experiences.

Many of the elderly experienced difficult times, such as serving in the military; some even fought in wars. Then there were stories about the Great Depression, the hardships in their families, which made them step up in their younger years to provide for their family. Some of the elderly population I encountered were immigrants who became proud American citizens and worked hard to make their way in an unfamiliar world. They chose to sacrifice much in order to journey into a new country for a new life. Some of the immigrants experienced unspeakable hardships and gave everything in order to flee to a land of hope called the United States of America. My four grandparents were strong immigrants that showed humility and love for America. They left the life they knew from Italy and ventured to America to become legal and proud citizens. Those stories interested me the most, and little did I know then that those stories helped mold the person I am today.

Prior to their journey to America, they planned to give their all and prove themselves worthy of this country. They spoke of how it was a privilege to become an American citizen. They communicated about their travels on a ship to Ellis Island in New York when they were children. They spoke about some of the hardships they endured and sometimes when they endured prejudice. But my grandparents never spoke as if they were victims, rather they spoke stories of victory and being grateful. There was always pride expressed when they spoke of their citizenship, their ventures, and their struggles. My four grandparents settled in the

Philadelphia area, worked hard to earn their pay, had stellar work ethic, which also instilled in my life. That work ethic, love of country, respect for others, and love of family trickled down into the upcoming generations in my family. If my grandparents were here today, I would honor them with praise and respect that is not understood when you are a child, but I understand it as an adult. I believe my grandparents knew what they were passing on to us and hoping it to be passed to generations after them. I would listen and learn by their stories and experiences that they shared with us. Like a sponge, I soaked up their stories. Their influence was part of what makes me who I am and who my family is. I see the interests that my own adult children show in their roots and ancestry. I believe the traditions and history of ancestry will continue to pass along to their children; I'm sure it will.

Throughout my years in my field of work, I treated many elderly patients in the hospital setting. I believe the oldest patient I had while working in the hospital was 106 years old. One of my workdays, he was on my list to visit and assess. I walked into his room and was astonished of how young he appeared to be. I would have guessed he was twenty years younger. I introduced myself to him, and I jokingly stated that I thought there was a typo on the paperwork; there was no way he was 106 years old. He laughed at me and said that he was 106 years old and that this was his first time in the hospital. He told me that he was healthy and hardly ever saw a doctor and that he was never sick until recently.

"I never needed a doctor until recently," he emphatically stated to me.

"I need to know your secrets for a long healthy life and how you look so young," I quipped back to him.

He jokingly said to me, "I run after girls, and I bet I can catch you."

We both laughed. His smile never left his dear face. He was as entertaining as he was interesting. These is the type of people that made my workday brighter and lighter.

Throughout my years in the hospital, I noticed that the elderly were the people that saw life as it was, whether it was good or bad. They would accept it and make the best of it. I did not hear them speak of their hard times as if they were victims, but rather it was always a story of how they were victorious, how they overcame difficult circumstances. In particular, I am awed by the elderly who were veterans, especially those who fought in war and survived terrible circumstances that are known as history. Most of my elderly patients didn't ask the staff for much. They accepted the moment and had less needs. I would remind elderly patients to please ask us for anything, that we were here to help and take care of their needs. The reply I usually received was that they didn't want to bother the staff, that they would be fine. I would look compassionately into their eyes and sincerely reply that they were not bothering us, that we were here to care for them. I would ask them to make a promise that they would not hesitate to ask for anything. Usually, they were set in their ways and lived as they believed. Their strength and dignity shined through their faces. Their hearts could be seen through their eyes. I would leave their rooms, wishing I could spend more time with them. I usually felt like they were my very own grandparents, and I wanted to take care of them in that manner. My heartstrings were tugged when it was time to leave my elderly patients' rooms. Often tears would show in my eyes, and some of those folks noticed it but would reassure me that they were fine.

Another morning at work, I was asked to evaluate an elderly gentleman who was going home on hospice. I had to evaluate his oxygen needs by titrating the amount of oxygen and record the findings so the doctor could write a prescription for home oxygen. I entered his room, announced who I was as I approached his bedside, and informed him of the short testing I needed to do. He was appropriate and aware. He appeared frail and weak but not in distress. He was in bed, partially sitting up, maybe at a forty-five-degree angle. There was a noticeable amount of increased work of breathing when he spoke, so his sentences were short, and he would pause at times. Right away I noted how kind his blue eyes were despite some cloudiness due to age, but his eyes were lovely. Despite his weakened and frail state, he was smiling. He had a polite gentleman effect, just like most of the men who were of that generation.

I explained that I knew he was going home this morning and that the physician would order the correct amount of oxygen needed for his home use. He kept staring at me. That frail smile remained on his face. He told me that he was so happy because he knew he was going home.

"I just want to go home one last time," he said to me. He was aware of his medical condition, his futile prognosis, and that is why he used the words "one last time." I am guessing he wanted to let me know, in case I wasn't aware, that he was going to be on hospice care at his home.

I informed him that I respected his wishes and would help him in whatever we could do for him to make his transport comfortable and get him home as quickly as we were able. He was glad to hear that the oxygen would be set up at home before his arrival. The testing went well. It did not take long to do and get the results. I explained that the test was complete, and I was going to give the physician the results so we could get things in place for him to leave as soon as possible. He looked at me with appreciation and seemed glad.

I know he saw the tears accumulating in my eyes as I leaned in to hold his hand. We stared at each other. It was difficult, but I held back crying. My heart hurt for him. He thanked me for helping him and said it again, "I just want to go home one last time."

I gently squeezed his hand and said that we were going to get this in motion immediately. He nodded, still smiling, his eyes never looking away from my eyes. I let him know that it was my pleasure to help with his need and that he made my day brighter just by meeting him. As I began to turn toward the door, I heard his soft weak voice once again, saying thank you. It took energy for him just to speak those words. It was difficult for me to walk away and to hold back tears, but I held it together. This circumstance with this dear patient raised a memory when my own maternal grandpop was weak and frail due to illness. But there were times he managed to speak a few words to me despite the difficulty it took for him to speak at all. My grandpop's last words to me were "I love you, baby dear." It took all he had to speak those words, but those words were just for me.

I stood outside the door in the hallway to finish a few notes and pull my thoughts together. The physician who took care of this dear man was walking by and stopped when he saw me. He walked over to get my report and told me he would get that order done right away. He expressed compassion and urgency because he wanted this man to get home as soon as possible this morning. The physician thanked me and asked me if I was okay. He saw the sadness in my face and was compassionate toward me. He stated that his patient was quite a man, and he was glad to help him get home, to fulfill his last wish. I was happy as well that we helped him get home one last time.

Chapter 11

2020: When the World Stood Still but First Responders Did Not

I grew up and also raised my four children in a small town on an island in South Jersey called the Wildwoods. It's a seashore community that has beautiful beaches, scenic views, lots of entertainment in the summer season, which also attracts tourism during the warm weather. In the colder weather, the little island grows quiet, and we are fortunate to essentially have good neighbors that live there year-round. My children and I all attended the schools on this resort island, and to this day, we talk about how much we cherished the teachers we had and the warm feeling of community.

Through the years, I observed the dedication of men and women who worked in the fire and police departments. And to this day, these departments have employed personnel that are stellar and dedicated. I'm proud to say that members of my own family were part of the fire and the police departments in those days. Today, there are still family and also friends and their extended families that continue serving in these departments. The influx of tourism in the summer season adds increased volumes to their rescues and 911 calls, as well as other workloads that are part of their jobs. The rides on the boardwalks, the ocean, and bay waters and huge amounts of tourists vastly increase the workloads and risks of our fire and police personnel. They are a great team of dedicated men and women that deserve praise and recognition not only in their work but also in their camaraderie in the community. These are the type of dependable and reliable people that help form great communities and give a sense of security to where you live. Though I wasn't a fan of the influx of tourism in the summer months, I never intended to move from my little island, my home for more than sixty-two years, where my roots were deeply imbedded in the beach sand.

In 2014, I was sensing in my heart to maybe make some changes in my life and perhaps to make a new start. At this time, I also chose to grow in relationship with God and was feeling a little restless about making life-changing decisions. I pondered as to whether or not to sell my home and live closer to one of my children and their family in Pennsylvania. They lived in the county of Lancaster, an area I loved visiting. So I traveled there often since a part of my family was living there. I have been an empty nester for quite a while. The kids were grown and on their own. It was me and my dog now. Even though I was content in my home and area that I lived in, I started to consider a change. I was an independent middle-aged woman still working a full-time job in a community hospital about a half hour away from where I lived. Most of my family and friends lived in this area as well. I'm certain that any decision I make would be life-changing if I were to dig up my roots and move from my home, which held wonderful memories and a feeling of security. I decided to pray about this, left it in God's hands for answers, and put it out of my mind for now.

Years passed, it was now 2020, and I was still working full-time in the hospital. At this time, I have been working in the community hospital in the county just minutes away from where I lived. I sold my house at the same time that I took employment in the community hospital, where I was familiar with the staff and personally knew people who worked there. Many of the patients that I saw in the hospital were familiar to me or I knew them personally. Some days, while working, I would encounter or even treat friends, family, acquaintances, former teachers, and employers that were now patients. It could be a bittersweet feeling to work in a place that was close to home. You never knew who you might see in your workday and under what circumstances that might arise. As for the patients that I knew personally, they seemed to welcome my familiar face in their hospital stay or trip to the emergency department. Some of the patients who knew me mentioned that they felt comfort seeing me, that a familiar face had given them a sense of relief. I can understand how that would be because hospitals can be an intimidating experience when you are a patient.

It was now January 2020, some news about a nouveau coronavirus was starting to trickle in from around the world. During our workday, we sought to find information about this virus that was creating such a mystery and increasing people's fears and uncertainties. We would question our physicians in our daily workday in hopes of finding out what this virus was all about. We didn't have much knowledge about this new virus, so essentially, we continued our normal functions in our hospital. Not much changed at this time in the way we worked. Discussions among us started to increase daily about this virus. We were questioning and repeating news we might have heard about. We shared news from media sources or the CDC or government. Since our hospital was located in South Jersey, perhaps we were feeling a little safer due to our location. Some of us were wondering if the virus would reach South Jersey at all. Then reports of the virus were spreading to all parts of the world. The virus was now spreading abundantly in areas including North Jersey and New York. Maybe we would be okay here. We were sort of secluded in our area. And this was the winter, so not many tourists traveled to our shoreline this time of year. Perhaps we wouldn't see that COVID at all in our small hospital.

The days were not too bad at the beginning of COVID. Then we began to see some changes made inside the hospital building. Certain units, such as the ICU and the unit nearby, were undergoing construction. It was looking like a MASH unit, just like what you saw on television. These areas were going to be used for patients that were infected with COVID because it was designed for isolation and set up for negative pressure, which was recommended in the medical world. The work progressed to the very floors we walked on, and we felt as if we were walking on a map of some sort. The flooring and seating that were looking like something that came out of a board game. Arrows were pasted on the floors to direct us into areas that were deemed isolation for donning or doffing the isolation PPE (personal protection equipment). Some of the arrows were strategically placed about six feet from each other because we had to sit and eat in the designated distances. That did not make sense to many of us because we treat patients as we stand shoulder to shoulder, crowded in patient rooms at any given time. There were signs on doors and walls that instructed and directed you to other signs and areas. There were so many signs everywhere that instructed you or warned you. We were instructed to wear masks, gowns, face shields, goggles, hair coverings that are now commonly being called PPE. We received instructions on how to don and doff the PPE we used and had special containment trash cans where we disposed contaminated PPEs. Many of us noted that our PPE was made in China.

Oh, geez, it just doesn't get better than that. The gowns were made from cheap material that resembled the wraps that covered a spring roll from a sushi bar. We were also issued masks that were made from some kind of disposable surgical material. We were instructed that these masks were not to be thrown away; instead, they were collected and bought to be disinfected and reused over and over again until they fell apart. I would unwrap these disinfected masks that had my name on it and noted how they smelled like chemicals. The smell was strong and undesirable. We hated to use them, but there were not much choices. The chemical smell would linger in my nose even after I removed the masks. Many of us wondered if the masks that were treated with chemical were going to make us ill; after all, it covered your nose and mouth throughout the day. Breathe in, breathe out, breathe in, breathe out. This was the beginnings when the rationing of PPEs started. But from what I understand, we were more fortunate than other facilities where medical personnel had even less PPEs. We appreciated the many generous and concerned citizens that donated constructed masks made from fabric to the medical staff. It was a kind showing of support, and we appreciated those masks that were handmade with colorful cheerful materials. Generosity from other citizens and groups were appreciated as well. Donations of food, goodies, toiletries, thank-you cards, prayers were all welcomed, and we appreciated all of it. At this point of the pandemic, we still were not aware of the caliber of change that was happening, not only to our little hospital but to the entire world. But suddenly we found out.

We began to receive some COVID-positive patients coming in through the emergency department. The very sick who needed the intensive care unit (ICU) were sent there, while others went into COVID-isolation units with the negative pressure capacity. Visitors were no longer permitted to enter the hospitals to be with their loved ones. The staff had deep compassion for our patients because of the restrictions and intense isolation. They had to endure not having family with them. The ICU is also the unit where patients who were on ventilators remained until they were weaned off ventilators or are taken off ventilators due to their demise. Respiratory therapists are the personnel that maintains patients on ventilators. We place patients on ventilators while we care for them and treat them throughout the amount of time needed and then remove patients from the ventilators. Our hopes are that when someone has to be on a ventilator that it will be a short-term treatment for them. But during the pandemic, we saw vented patients remain on ventilators longer. During the beginnings of COVID, ventilators were the main choice of treatment to those that were critically ill, who tested COVID positive. Day by day, the number of patients admitted to the hospital increased, the workloads were getting heavier, and so was the stress and anxieties in everyone.

Each day that we clocked in to the hospital, we were bombarded by the word *COVID*. It was a steady and constant overwhelming word used on every patient. From the time a patient entered the hospital, they had their nose swabbed to test for COVID. And if you test positive, you now became a COVID statistic. We still were not sure about the transmission of this virus or if everybody was going to catch it and die from it. We were continually questioned by patients and families, but many of those questions did not have an answer since this was new to everyone around the world. The news reports were on, twenty-four hours a day. The reports of deaths all over the world were depicted on the TV screen, as if we were counting down to the end of time, as if it were an Armageddon. Reality was setting into everyone in the medical field, and we were also beginning to question if we were going to be doomed as a civilization. Sometimes those thoughts alone added immensely to the large amounts of stress that we experienced. But we chose to keep doing what we were trained to do, and that was to care for the sick. The sick people in the hospital setting were becoming plentiful, and not many of them were getting discharged to go home. In fact, their hospital stays were extended due to COVID testing and their illness. We were running out of patient rooms, which hospitals worldwide had the same issues. Our community hospital was beginning to make plans to set up an extended unit attached to the hospital to accommodate the overflow of patients. After all, no one knew when this nightmare was going to end and if it would end.

There was a period of time that our medical personnel were increasingly becoming sick with the virus. Day by day, one, two, or three staff members called out sick because of being ill with the virus. Short staffing in the hospitals and nursing homes became a common problem seen worldwide. Management would sometimes plead with staff to take more overtime, and many of us did. Finally, we were offered some bonus money when we took overtime. The organizations referred to it as bonus money. The staff referred to it as patronizing ———. It was an insulting small fee, considering the risks and workload that we endured, especially when you were hearing news reports of medical personnel who died from the virus from all around the world. The small bonuses certainly did not compensate the increased workloads and risks, but we had a job to do. we needed to care for sick people, and that is what first responders did. We did our job and didn't quit. Despite the unknowns, we continued to work. The flavor of the condescending bonuses tasted worse when we became aware that hospitals were receiving extra monies from the government when patients received a COVID diagnosis. It is bad enough that we don't receive pensions or medical packages on retirement, so now it adds insult to the injury. *Gee, thanks a lot. Hello, so what about us? Now, because of COVID, the risks in our jobs have now increased exponentially. We are on the front lines of an unknown viral pandemic, and we are working harder and short staffed. So keep singing your praises to us and calling us heroes,* which none of that was compensation. In fact, at times, it sounded condescending. To make things worse, some of the sick personnel unknowingly brought the virus home, and it infected their families. I was fortunate to live on my own because if I did get the virus, it would not be shared at my house, and I don't think my dog would have been infected. As far as I know, I don't think I was infected with COVID. And if I was, I didn't have the classic symptoms associated with the virus. I called out of work just one day due to stomach flu–like symptoms, but otherwise I did not experience anything worse than that, except being fatigued at times.

The days continued, as if you were watching a rerun of a bad television show. You would arrive at work, mask up before you entered the building, record your body temperature to make sure there was no fever, and then answer the same questions regarding whether you had symptoms or not each and every day. We were screened each day; it was part of the new routine. And each time you heard of someone being ill, you immediately asked if they had COVID. In fact, we were wondering if there were any of the regular flu and seasonal colds existing at this time. No, everything seemed to be centered around COVID. If you tested negative, you would enter into the department and receive report, plan your priorities, then shift from first to fourth gear. The adrenaline would start to flow. Walking and running to emergency and other calls we received was tiresome due to wearing the masks that were constantly on our face, making our breathing abnormal and a feeling of smothering. There was a time that we were instructed to also use a surgical mask and wear it over the N95 mask. This was done when it involved certain procedures that had droplet precautions, such as suctioning, administering CPAP machines, intubations (breathing tube insertion), and extubations (breathing tube taken out). The N95 masks had to be fit tested, so you needed to know your size that you were going to wear, and then you were to use that size N95 each time. N95 masks fit tighter to your face than a regular surgical mask, and they were thicker, which made it harder to breathe. I'm one of those middle-aged women who get hot flashes, so this now became more of an irritating time to get hot and sweat while wearing PPE.

At the end of my shift, I would wash up, clock out, exit the building, then you were permitted to remove your mask once you were outside the building. As soon as I walked through those doors, I would whip off the mask and start sucking in the fresh air. It felt as good as those times that I would breathe in the scent of fresh summer rain on a summer day; it was sweet and clear. I would walk to the parking lot, lean against my car for a few minutes, and continue taking slow, long, deep breaths. I would catch the delightful scent of the sea air, which was refreshing and soothing. I would close my eyes and slowly take in this pleasure. I sometimes would stare up into the sky and just take in the feeling of freedom to be outside. I was unequivocally thankful to God that I was not a COVID statistic that had to remain inside hospital walls. Once again, I was going home. My drive home was just minutes away. How much I looked forward to seeing my dog and getting a shower. I would then get into my car and start to back out of the parking spot, looking in the rearview mirror as I backed out again, noting that the reflection of my face looked the same each time. There were dents, bumps, and bruises all over my face, especially under my eyes and on the bridge of my nose, which had raw skin, which was a result of wearing the N95 masks. My face looked nasty and unattractive, but my dog would be happy when I get home no matter what I looked like.

Chapter 12

Will This Pandemic Continue?

Rise and shine to another workday, my alarm clock was blaring away at 4:45 a.m. It was dark outside. The chill of the winter weather enticed me to fall back to sleep, and it was still COVID pandemic time. Maybe something great would occur today, and we would get news that the pandemic is over so we could resume life prior to this nightmare. I don't think it would be today.

I crawl quietly out of bed, being careful not to wake up my dog. I like to let her sleep a while longer. She is elderly and sleeps more often. I washed up, dressed, and sat down in front of my lighted mirror to put on some make up as I usually do each morning. Why put on makeup when you spend a twelve-hour shift wearing masks that cover most of your face? one might ask. My answer is that I wanted to feel as normal as possible, which was difficult for any of us to find normal lately. It was important for me to make my eyes look nice. I wanted my eyes to look as pretty as possible because that was the only area that was not covered by a mask while I was at work. When I walked into a patient's room, I wanted them to see my eyes so they knew I was looking at them while I approached them. It's important to me that they saw my eyes looking at their eyes and that they had my attention. The eyes can give an immediate message of expression. And as for me, it was important that my patients could see that I cared for them and that I had compassion for them. It was difficult enough for our patients to hear us speak through those masks, which surely muffled our voices as we communicate to our patients.

My hair routinely is put into a ponytail and held together by a headband to keep stray hair from getting into my face. You don't want to brush your hair away from your face while you are working; your hands may contaminate yourself with germs when you touch your face. I truly believe that most of the virus transmissions were caused by contaminated hands because I witnessed many colleagues that manipulated their masks while working. I started to observe people in general and noticed who scratched their noses, rubbed their eyes, used tissues to wipe their noses without washing their hands first. Most of those people became ill due to the virus. I had questioned myself if I washed my hands well enough prior to putting on and taking off my masks, especially now that workloads increased, and we were working at a faster pace. In our jobs, we keep moving from patient to patient, task to task, and hand sanitizing sometimes flounders in between. We don't intentionally neglect hand sanitizing; however, we move too quickly during the workday because that is what the job requires—get it done; get it done now. If you started to take a break to eat or drink, and you got a STAT call, you had to don up the PPE, return your mask on your face, and run to the call. Did I wash my hands well enough, or did I touch something contaminated prior to putting on my mask? Many days I would clock out, go home, and then when it was time to relax or go to sleep, I found myself recalling the events of my workday and if I might have contaminated myself due to mask changing or repositioning my mask. I would rerun the scenarios of donning and doffing the PPE throughout the day and if I possibly contaminated myself. My times of relaxing and trying to get to sleep should not be the time to think about all this, so I needed to stop thinking of it each night. I don't think I ever stopped thinking about it, especially when it was time to unwind. Thoughts were difficult to turn off, as if you would flip a switch.

One last look in the mirror, and I decided my makeup looked okay. Soon it was time to drive to work. Sometimes, while I get ready for work, a feeling of dread would start to emerge, and I would find myself starting to sob a little and wish I did not have to go to work. What the heck was going on? This dreaded feeling was happening now and then. I didn't like this rude interference. I didn't like that there were times in the morning I would sometimes have tears well up in my eyes because I was dreading another day to work in this messy pandemic. But I had to work, so I would turn off those thoughts once again and get moving along. Besides, I didn't want to mess up my eye makeup. There was no time to waste in the early morning hours. My feelings of dread were sometimes accompanied by feelings of fear caused by this pandemic. I refuse to let fear control me, so I would talk to God and ask Him to chase away my fears. Sometimes I would sing hymns or listen to worship music while I dressed for work, which helped me get through those negative thoughts. Time to finish up and attend to my dogs' needs then get on my way. This was my routine of how I got ready for work day after day.

Months later, I realized how conditioned I became due to the constant reminders of wearing masks and following PPE protocols. Repetition and reactions that occurred in jobs such as in the medical field seem to unknowingly carry out into your personal life as well. I was beginning to catch myself reacting by the behavior learned while I was on the clock and working. A few times that I was driving alone in my car and waiting at a red light, another car pulled up next to mine. I would unknowingly and reactively reach for my mask and was about to put it on my face. Yep, that is what I said. I reached for my mask and was about to put it on my face because a car with people pulled up next to me. What a strange reaction that was. I realized I became conditioned to reach for masks when a person or people approached me. The behavior was reactive and subconscious, as if I were a Pavlovian dog. The last time this incidence occurred, I became upset and angry at the same time to this reaction. "Oh my goodness, this is not good. I'm not going to become someone who has transitioned into a sub-human being." Humans are not meant to be conditioned, that is not what freedom is about. In that moment of tears and fears, I decided that this is not the way I am going to continue my life. I then made a decision to become free from this instilled behavior. So I gave it to God. I asked Him to free me from this conditioned behavior, to strengthen me, to release me from any fears that I might have. I didn't think I feared any of this; after all, we were all on the front lines while we worked in this COVID environment. I began to realize that the health and well-being of medical personnel can be affected by how we were trained and how we work in our job. I was trained to automatically put on masks if I had to approach a person or if a person approached me. It had now become a reaction and not a thought, and it was carrying into my off-the-clock time in my personal life. I prayed about this behavior and the fears that accompanied it. My job is a part of my life; it is not all of my life.

It wasn't too long that the feeling of freedom of fears and the conditioned behaviors that started to turn around into normal behavior became liberating for me. Despite the constant and consistent demands that continued to bombard us in our workday, I continued to pray and think about conquering fears and resuming my normal. We were impacted with negativity and fears via the media, the government, CDC, and other sources. I decided that I was going to grasp whatever normal that I could make happen. I was going to start to socialize with my family, especially with my grandchildren. I would begin to socialize with friends and take part in group activities, despite the implementation of mandates from this chaos. None of us knew what the outcome of this pandemic was going to be and if all of our lives may be cut short. And by the way, to all of you who were commanding us to live a certain way, to be locked down and obey mandates, it was noticed that you were not following your own rules, so don't tread on me.

> You will know the truth, and the truth will make you free. (John 8:32)

> He who speaks truth, tells what is right, but a false witness, deceit. (Proverbs 12:17)

> For God has not given us a spirit of timidity, but of power and love and discipline. (2 Timothy 1:7)

Have I not commanded you? Be strong and courageous! Do not tremble or be dismayed, for the Lord your God is with you wherever you go. (Joshua 1:9)

Chapter 13

2020—Most Patients Went Home

The pandemic continued to cripple the world. The hospitals were overwhelmed by sick patients, and medical personnel staffing was still disproportionate to the workloads. Worldwide, everyone was hurting in some form. Many people were losing the hope that we may survive as a civilization. Many of our patients in the hospital would oftentimes ask us, "How long will it take until I go home?" Unfortunately, none of us had that answer, or the answer might differ due to the updated CDC and government rulings. We continued to reassure and encourage each patient and each other, giving rise to any optimism that came forth, hoping for the best that was yet to come.

At this time at the hospital, during the pandemic, we mostly saw patients that recovered from the virus and went home. When a COVID patient was about to be discharged, many of the employees would line up in the hallways to wave and say their goodbyes to that patient. The doors in the unit would open; a transporter would be pushing the patient who sat in a wheelchair. As they made their way to the lobby to check out of the building, the employees who were present would clap their hands, wave, and express their heartfelt goodbyes. It made for a nice send-off for the patients. It was as if they won the battle of the COVID, and now they had freedom to leave the building. I'm certain that the patients that went home were smiling, but we couldn't see it because the masks they had to wear covered their nose and mouth.

I was assigned to the ICU many times, as we all were. Essentially, we worked together in every unit because more than ever, it took teamwork. Ventilators were our main job, and the ICU had ventilators in almost every room, and the need for them was growing. In those times of the pandemic, the treatments of how to manage patients infected with this virus was not fully known, so many patients were attached to ventilators longer due to the uncertainties and the severity of their illness. The sickest of the patients were those with comorbidities, such as obesity, diabetes, and hypertension, as well as the elderly. Different methods and therapies for ventilator patients became new to us. Proning is a term that required a team of people to slowly turn a patient onto their stomach, which helped with their oxygenation and ventilation. It was a turning technique that had to be synchronized by a team of us so we could safely turn a patient. The majority of these patients were attached to the ventilator and to numerous tubes and wires. Proning a patient required at least six of us to safely perform this therapy. Once you proned a patient, you would become a little more confident with each subsequent proning. But nevertheless, it was a daunting task. The outcomes of this therapy were showing positive results in critical patients, so we were glad to be part of the team that did the proning, despite how time consuming it was.

Worldwide, it was difficult times for medical personnel that treated patients each day. Being understaffed and overworked became the norm in hospitals and nursing homes. There were little times when you could get a break, which made for a happy moment just for the fact that you could remove your mask to eat or drink something even while you were on the run. Keeping hydrated, especially because we wore masks that seemed to make us more thirsty, and eating nutritiously was not easy to fit in your day. Grab-and go-foods were made for an easier option but not a sensible nutritious one. I don't know of anyone who wasn't glad when the shift was over, and it was time to clock out, get home to eat a good meal with their loved ones. We all appreciated and were grateful that we could go home; however, we felt compassion for the patients that had to stay in the hospital until they were well enough to go home. The environment that was created in the hospitals and nursing facilities due to COVID was depressing and very frightening. I had my own thoughts of what it would be like if I or one of my loved ones had to be in the hospital at this time due to the pandemic, and it was a frightening thought. Those of us who were able to go home at the end of another shift would feel the happy and freeing moment when we swiped that badge and clocked out. Many times, I would clock out, leave the building, and get upset, knowing there were patients who could not leave but wanted to leave due to how frightened they were. I personally knew some of those patients, and it would add to my sad feelings.

One afternoon, my presence was requested by a patient in the ICU. He wanted to talk with the respiratory therapist. I wasn't sure what he wanted prior to walking in his room, but I donned up the PPE and slowly opened the sliding glass door. Sitting up in bed was a middle-aged gentleman. He was alert and oriented, but I noted moderate labored breathing. He was attached to what we refer to as a high-flow oxygen device. I introduced myself. And while I looked at him and the monitor, I could see I needed to increase his oxygen to a higher percentage, which I immediately did. He was able to speak in short sentences without further distress. So while I listened to him, I would glance at the monitor at the same time to make sure his oxygen status and vitals were okay. He expressed his main concern to me, which was that he wanted to go home. He said he wanted oxygen to be delivered to his home, and he was willing to pay for it. His eyes were locked on my eyes as he spoke with me. The expression on his face and the tone of his voice verified my belief that he was frightened.

This was going to take a careful and concise explanation in as simple terms as I could express to inform this dear man. My heart hurt for him. There was absolutely no way he could leave the hospital and survive at home. His status was critical. He wouldn't be able to survive the time it would take for him to leave this building. I began to explain why he was in the ICU and that it was not just because he had COVID but because he was in critical condition, and the medical treatment he needed could only be given in the ICU. When I completed my explanation, he continued to talk about oxygen. He kept believing that if he could just get oxygen in his home that he would get well at home. Once again, I explained it to him while I showed compassion and understanding in my explanation. I informed him that we would give him the best of care, and we were doing everything medically that was needed for him. I truly felt the desperation that this man was trying to convey to me. He realized how sick he was, plus the fear that this pandemic caused was enough to make people feel isolated and that death would be eminent.

I could see it in his eyes that this man was still scared. The feeling of fear emanated, and nothing I could say would change that. I let him know that

I was going to speak to the physician at this time, and I squeezed and held his hand. I tried to reassure him that we were doing everything possible to make him well. The fright in his eyes was still obvious to me. His expression did not change. I turned to exit his room, and then I spoke with the physician. Shortly afterward, the physician spoke with this gentleman, but the feeling of anxiety and fear remained with this patient. Each time I walked past his room while I continued my work, I would look at him and nod, hoping that some assurance would lessen his fears. At the end of the shift, I stood in front of the closed glass doors to look at him one more time prior to clocking out. I nodded to him. I raised up my hand, as if to wave goodbye. I believe my eyes spoke the compassion that I had in my heart for him. He nodded in return, but his eyes did not change. Fear was still with him. His eyes told the story, and I felt sad for him. I exited the ICU, gave report, clocked out, then drove home. But this dear man who desperately wanted to go home had to remain in the ICU.

The next morning, I returned to the ICU for another workday. I received report that during the night, this gentleman was intubated and put on a ventilator. His prognosis became very poor. I entered his room to check on him and the ventilator. He was asleep due to sedation. The monitor and ventilator confirmed that he took a turn for the worse. Hours later, while he was still on the ventilator, he succumbed to death.

Chapter 14

2020, the Year of Change

Somewhere around spring, we were starting to see a bit of relief in the hospital setting. COVID patients were still being hospitalized and treated, and most patients were still getting discharged to go home. New techniques in patient care and new medications were implemented for patients infected with COVID, as well as new information learned from around the world. The warmer weather was enticing people to get outdoors, and we were all ready to escape the demands for the world to be locked down. No one wants to be mandated to be locked inside their homes, to be told they should not participate in holiday gatherings, and to wear masks all the time, especially the mandates that were put on children. Some of us noticed that there were government officials that weren't abiding by their own rules, and yet they were forcing society into isolation. It isn't normal for humans to live this way, and many people chose to start living in freedom.

We are now hearing the increased evidence about the damaging effects that the lockdowns had on society in the entire world; it is sad and abnormal.

The sense of some relief was felt during these workdays. We were starting to see the light through the darkness. The isolations and precautions were still in effect during our shifts at the hospital. We had adapted to our surroundings and the way things were inside the hospital walls. It's not that we were happy about it, but we settled into the fact that we had to work under certain conditions. At least now we were believing that there was hope ahead. No one wants to give up hope. The feeling of expectation in something good to happen is innate in humans. Unfortunately, there were those who did give up because of this pandemic and the lockdowns. It is estimated that in 2020, deaths from drugs, alcohol, and suicide largely increased in the United States. COVID mandates severely impacted everyone; some were affected in extreme ways. Many of those stories are known throughout the world, and I do not believe the stories will ever end. This is history that will not be forgotten.

During the summer of 2020, I began to consider taking a step in another direction. Then not too long after, I made life-changing decisions. I sold my home by the beach about a year prior, and now I was contemplating making a move away from New Jersey and relocating to Lancaster, Pennsylvania. I put that in prayer as well in 2014, and now I was believing it was time for this move, a move that would leave my family and friends behind with all that I ever knew, everything that was familiar and comfortable to me. I felt the tugging in my heart and knew it was time to leave, so I packed up my life possessions, found an apartment in a lovely area called Lititz, Pennsylvania, which was not too far from one of my daughters and her family. By the end of 2020, I moved to Lancaster, Pennsylvania, with my dog and pretty much everything I owned. It was a bittersweet time because I knew I would miss my New Jersey family. But it was exciting, knowing that I was going to spend more time with my Pennsylvania family and to venture into a new journey. I admit that I was a little bit scared, but I believed in my heart, I needed to do this.

I settled in an area that seemed to be suitable for me, a central location which gave me opportunities to find a job that was nearby to where I was now living. It was my hope to find a respiratory therapist job, but I did not want to work in a hospital anymore. After twenty-five years in the hospital setting, I wanted to try a different route. Even though I am a healthy person for the most part, I realized that I was experiencing symptoms that I was ignoring prior to my move to Pennsylvania. I was believing that this past year, working in the hospital during COVID was the turning point of not wanting any more hospital jobs. It is difficult to explain about all those symptoms I was experiencing, but I realized they were there. I was not addressing their existence like I should because I am a health-conscious person and believed that I could push through it. Looking back at all of it, along with the symptoms I experienced, I also realized I was sleeping less than usual, and I was not a person who slept much anyway. I believed I didn't need normal sleep because I always functioned well, and I didn't get sick much. Now my mind and body constantly felt like it was in overload and fast-paced. It was challenging for me to relax and unwind, as if a steady flow of adrenaline was running through my veins. I appeared to look okay outwardly. I would function normally, but the symptoms I was experiencing was not okay. I still lead a healthy lifestyle of good nutrition and exercise, but I could not slowdown in mind and body. My symptoms manifested and were getting worse. I now had heart palpitations that would not cease, which also caused anxiousness, and I became concerned. I needed to get a checkup by a physician, so I made that appointment and was sent to a couple specialists. After blood work, heart monitor, and other diagnostic testing, it was concluded that my heart was healthy, and my other tests were fine. I took my time looking for a new job, learned to relax a little more, and prayed. The symptoms began to subside, and I was starting to feel more like myself again.

In the spring of 2021, I was hired by a nursing home near the area that I now live. It was fortunate for me that there were no COVID vaccine mandates required there, because after careful consideration, I am not getting this vaccine. Through my years, I chose to get many vaccines. I chose the ones that made sense to me. But I believe that living a healthy lifestyle is the key to fighting off many diseases. There were colleagues I knew personally that were losing jobs due to the vaccine mandates, and many of us experienced ridicule and were demonized for not accepting the COVID vax. We, the medical personnel that were called heroes, were now being treated by the government and some others as if we were zeroes and an outcast in society. It was a relief for me to now be employed in a job that accepted employees that declined the vaccine. Grateful am I again.

Working Monday through Friday instead of twelve-hour shifts was a change in itself, and I soon adapted to a slower pace of working. This nursing home was different from other nursing facilities that I visited. First of all, the location was scenic. It is located on top of a hill, surrounded by other hills, valleys, and farmland. My drive to this facility bought delight to me because of the scenery that consisted of farms, animals, creeks, and horse-drawn buggies. I love the warmth and beauty of countryside, the tenderness of heart that it gives me. The staff employed at the nursing facility were hardworking people, and they were welcoming to me. The staff were caring and friendly to the residents who lived in this facility. Within a short time, I was grateful to work with these wonderful folks and felt a belonging and sense of family. The atmosphere inside the facility was one that was warm, peaceful, and spiritual. My job was slow-paced, basic, and straightforward. I was in a good place for sure, so grateful am I once again.

Soon after my employment, I became acquainted with the long-term residents and the staff of caretakers in this facility. The elderly residents that resided there were the sweetest people. I knew them by their names and faces. Yes, most of the time, I saw those lovely people unmasked because masking was not a big issue as far as the residents were concerned. There were certain precautions taken, but for the most part, the residents could not tolerate wearing masks twenty-four hours daily. We did experience additional COVID breakouts several times while I was employed there. Though it was not the same scenario that we went through in the early parts of 2020. It still had impacted the way these dear folks lived. I was fond of these lovely residents. And of course, seeing some of them sick and some die added more sorrow to my heart. These elderly folks were ones that I will not forget. Most of them worked hard prior to their need of a nursing facility. Some of the residents endured hardships, and most of them had a lifetime of working hard while raising their families. Despite living through all kinds of circumstances, and now they were needing nursing care, they smiled much of the time. These residents were friendly and loved having visitors. Most of them enjoyed quiet activities. And once the COVID rules became more relaxed, they were able to get outdoors. I found most of them to have a beautiful spirit, and it warmed my heart each and every workday. It was a pleasure to go to work. I have a respiratory therapist job that had a lower stress level, and I can usually walk instead of always running while I worked here.

We once again had a COVID breakout and another isolation time that we were busy. Some of the residents were now ill, and there were some residents that had the virus but had little or no symptoms. Most of them recovered and did well; a few of these dear folks died. The residents who died were the ones that had comorbidities or were very old. On one of the days, during the COVID isolations, I recall one gentleman who was very ill. But as frail and weak as he was, he wanted to sit in his chair to read his Bible. I entered his room to assess him, noting immediately how very weak he was. He was sitting in his chair and leaning forward, resting his arms on a little table in front of him. There were a few personal items on the table, including a Bible. He told me that he could not find his eyeglasses and that he would like to read his Bible. I began to search for the eyeglasses but could not find them, so I peered out his door to find his aide so she could help me search for the eyeglasses. She entered his room, and we both kept searching. We looked over and under everything in that room.

After searching for quite a long time, we explained to this dear man that we weren't going to give up and that we would return to look again. The aide was wondering if perhaps the eyeglasses might have been on a food tray or with linens, so she continued to search in other areas in that hallway. I was holding his hand. And with a weak voice, he told me, once his glasses were found, he wanted to read his Bible. I noted that his hands were now resting ever so gently on the pages of his Bible, which was opened in front of him. You can see in his eyes that he was determined to read. I knew that I needed to figure out something. I had a pair of my reading glasses with me that I use so I could see closer when I wrote notes during my assessments. I took them out of my pocket and gently put them on this lovely gentleman's face, being careful they weren't too tight around his ears and nose. Though he was weak and frail, a noticeable smile formed on his face. Through his weakness, he managed to lift his head to look at me and said, "Thank you" His voice was so frail, and he looked so tired; it broke my heart. He began to turn the pages of his Bible. It seemed to have lifted his spirits, as if he was given a treasure chest of gold. It meant that much to him to have some kind of eyeglasses so he could read his Bible. I don't know if those glasses helped his sight, but he stared at his Bible, and his hands lovingly and respectfully touched those pages. I stood there a while longer and asked him if he was okay and repeated that we would return to see him. My eyes began to fill with tears. I then squeezed his hand and told him that I prayed for him. Once again, with his weak shaky voice, he said, "Thank you." I could see and feel the peace and tranquility that emanated from this man. It made me feel better that he now looked content and happier. I slowly exited his room, hoping he would get many more days to read his Bible. Later that day, the staff phoned his family so they could speak with him. At this time, there was still no visitation due to the COVID mandates. I was told by the staff who took care of him that his family were loving and caring people. The family appreciated that the staff helped this dear man make the phone call so they were able to tell him how much they loved and missed him. It would be the last time they heard his voice, for he succumbed to death not long afterward.

I was fond of these lovely residents, and of course seeing some of them sick and some die added more sorrow in my heart. These elderly folk bought joy to my heart, and I enjoyed listening to their stories. Although many of them had dementia, they would tell me stories, and I loved listening to them. They had families and friends who cared for and loved them. For the most part, these folks accepted what life dealt to them and sustained their joy until the end. I won't forget all of you. A heart always remembers. So grateful am I once again.

We didn't let you die alone.

Mandates changed the rules. Hospitals and nursing homes shut out families from their loved ones, but we didn't let you die alone.

We couldn't take the place of your families, but we gathered around you while you were drifting away and succumbing to your death.

We whispered the words "We are here. Your family loves you" as your hands were held by those of us who stopped what we were doing so we could comfort you.

Your phone was used to call your loved ones so they could see and talk with you one last time.

We would hear them crying, telling you how much they missed you and love you.

Our hearts hurt for you. Your loved ones wanted to be with you, and we know you wanted them near.

We weren't your family, but we didn't let you die alone.

Chapter 15

How Do Caregivers Heal?

There are no quick fixes to heal anyone, and we are individuals who may require individual ways to heal up while we work years, even decades, in our jobs. Essentially, we need to practice good, healthy lifestyle, hopefully from the beginning of a young age so it will benefit our mind and body as we age. As a parent, I taught my children who are now adults the importance of good health and well-being while they were young. My four children are still maintaining a healthy lifestyle, and they are now the example for their children—proud mom moment.

A healthy lifestyle is a must do, a nonnegotiable. We must make some effort to nurture and maintain our bodies and minds as age progresses. There are techniques and therapies that we may implement to enhance and to help heal ourselves and help other people. I am happy to briefly share how I am still rolling with work stress and in general life stresses while maintaining a healthy lifestyle. We can maintain optimal health while living with stressful circumstances because we know that stress of some sort will be a constant in life. Since stressful situations will arise, the way we handle it is what we need to figure out so we can get through those times. The obstacles of life are a challenge that can make us stronger while we walk through it, or it can make us sick while going through it. The choices we make or sow for ourselves largely impact the results we reap.

For those of us who work in the same field of work as we do seem to understand and will empathize with each other. Most of us can read our coworkers' expressions and know they may need an ear to listen to them, so it is important and healing to just listen and be supportive. We all want to know we are valued, so be a listener, give a compliment or a compassionate word to all colleagues. Small helpful gestures can positively impact someone in large ways. Many of us also will assist our colleagues by helping them in a task, even if it was in a small way during a busy day. The best team players are the ones that would just show up, stating that they were checking on you and would then jump in and help you with a task. Part of being a team player is when you help your colleagues, whether in a large or small way, because taking care of patients is a team effort. I look back in the days that I worked jobs such as food serving, cosmetology, and housekeeping. I was taught by the employers of any job

I worked that camaraderie and teamwork applies to all jobs. I agree. I worked with some awesome team players and colleagues that I will cherish for life. I won't forget you and how you eased burdens and heavy loads during my workday by helping in a small or large way, but mostly because you were genuine in your efforts. Your heart shined, and I saw it each time.

First responders seem to share their work stories with other first responders. The camaraderie in this profession is sometimes unspoken but supportive in other ways. You just know when a coworker or a first responder in another field of work needs to vent or share an experience from their workday. We listen, show compassion, sometimes grieve with them, knowing they felt pain in some way. We seem to understand each other. I've shared stories within my own family because I have family members who are first responders. My family consists of firefighters/EMTs, police, nurses, a physician, and military. We have shared stories, spoken of similar emotions because of what we see and do. Occasionally, we throw in some advice or give words of encouragement and understanding to each other. There were moments we lighten up the conversations by making jokes or to challenge a "who can top this." My son-in-law, who is the physician, may call my other son-in-law, who is a firefighter, the hero. My son-in-law firefighter may quip to my son-in-law police officer that one day the officer's kids will grow up to be a firefighter, just like their uncle. It's all in fun. We make time to laugh a little. You definitely have to laugh, and I want to laugh more often. We try to get together as family, especially during the holidays, but it is difficult to gather together because of different workdays and shifts. Through the years, we would plan an alternative holiday so we can have celebrations as a family. It became a way of life that was accepted, and I cherish all of it.

Throughout the years, I also noticed that the camaraderie among the first responders and medical personnel became like family even outside the workplace. While working a twelve-hour shift, day after day, you may forge lasting friendships that may also become a family unit. You work and eat together. Many times bonds are formed for life. People may become an extension of your own family. It's nice to be part of people that understand you and have shared commonalities.

Sometimes, therapists, pastors, psychologists are helpful and needed if you decide that is a good method for solutions and self-help. Professional therapists and clergy can be an asset because they usually have an unbiased view of your life, and they can help lead you to solutions. A good, trusted friend, who will listen and support us, is sometimes all we need. I am blessed to have some in my personal circle. Talking and listening to each other is essential, as well as showing and receiving compassion, giving compliments and encouragement are all positive practices. People were not created to suppress and hold in emotions and problems. Essentially, we are social beings who need some nurturing and interactions from those that we trust.

What else can we do to keep ourselves well and healthy, both physically and mentally? As for my own experiences, I am a lifestyle-fitness person. As years pass, life holds challenges to keep your body and mind in shape. My job entails being physical, but I will always take time to exercise to benefit my body and mind. In my early years, I would be in the gym, working out in beast mode, challenging myself to grow physically stronger, flexible, and agile. I modified my exercise through the years because we do age, even though I still fight and sometimes deny that fact. It depends on how I feel prior to my workout or the type of workout I am going to do that day. I use weight-bearing methods to maintain strength, build bone density to help prevent osteopenia, osteoporosis, and bone fractures. I also implement cardio workouts, which is self-explanatory and is a must. If the weather is nice, I would take a run along the beach where I lived, and now I run along the park in my neighborhood. I like to enjoy my run by enjoying the outdoor scenery and fresh air. I monitor my heart rates to make sure I reach the target rates that are right for me. If the weather is colder, I enjoy the StairMaster in the rec center that I have a membership to. I do my own routines on the StairMaster to achieve a fuller body workout.

I'm not as agile like I was in my twenties, but I do pretty well for my age. So I exercise, challenging myself in a more moderate way. In my midtwenties, I actually considered myself somewhat of a workout beast. In those days, I was working a job as a cosmetologist. I would go to the gym prior to sunrise and work out and then began training for competition. After my workout, I would go home and get the kids ready for school and then go to work. I challenged myself to become physically stronger and decided to do a few physique competitions, which were fun, and I enjoyed the challenges. I was fortunate to be in a gym with other people that also had dedication to working out, and some of the guys and gals competed in various competitions. We would all support each other's goals, attend competitions together. It was a great time and good camaraderie.

I also do more exercises for balance, which I believe is beneficial as we age. Everybody, stretch! I believe stretching is beneficial for everyday activities. It helps with moving to fuller range of motion and increases blood flow. It feels so good to me after I concentrate on some stretching. Even when I am sitting, I will remind myself to do some stretching techniques. I start with my head and neck and eventually finish some stretching on the floor at my home. You don't have to be in the gym to do stretches, and some exercises can be done at home. There are so many options of exercising online, but be careful on how and what you choose to do.

Perhaps a consultation with a physician or instructors may be needed prior to what kind of exercises to do.

When someone says to me that they don't have the time to exercise, I sometimes suggest to begin working out at least three times weekly for thirty minutes. And if that is all you can do, then that is all you can do. You will still reap benefits from this. Then as you begin to feel the wonderful results of exercise, increase the amount of time and days until you are satisfied with what you are doing and how you feel. Tailor and customize until a balance of life is achieved that fits who you are. There is no need to achieve beast mode. Keep it simple and real for your life. I just want people to move, to feel better in their bodies and mind because exercise improves mind and body. We were not made to be dormant. God created a strong, unique machine in all of us. We just have to utilize it.

I am a believer of integrative care for myself. Checkups and some diagnostic testing are needed. And for me, alternative medicine and techniques are part of my personal care. I benefit from chiropractic therapy massage, physical therapies, and other natural therapies. I use some practical and quality nutritional supplements and vitamins. I am mindful of good hydration with water and sometimes using additives to water, such as electrolytes.

Nutritious food is a must. Don't consume just any foods that feel comforting or to make you feel full. I can write volumes about nutrition with food in itself. I completed a ten-month course to certify as a functional nutrition coach. I love giving information and coaching someone to reach good health for their own personal goals. In our country, food quality has decreased due to many reasons, such as processing and pollution. Also, we sometimes choose quick-food fixes because many of us are eating while being on the go. If there were no grocery stores on earth, what would you be eating? That's right, we would be eating off of the earth, the foods that God provided. I encourage people to reset your mind, and you will be healthier when you choose more natural foods. Disregard the marketing of processed feel-good or comfort foods because they are not good choices for our health. I aim to eat at least 85 percent clean, but I will set days aside for treats and some feel-good choices. But then, I get back on track of good nutrition. It is nice to have foods that make you feel good, maybe bring back good memories too. However, it may not be the healthiest of choices. I do grace myself at times to eat celebratory foods, especially on holidays. I do not drink alcoholic beverages very much, and I can't tolerate much of it anyway. Give yourself a comfort or fun food time, but get back on track with proper nutritious eating. You will reap the rewards of good health of body and mind and have a more optimal and quality life.

Being grateful for the smallest of things is rewarding, fulfilling, healing, and builds positivity. If those small things were no longer in existence, it would become a big problem. Turning on a faucet for water seems like a small thing. Flipping a switch for electricity seems like a small thing. I had days that the electric was out or the water lines froze; they were the days that I was reminded of how important those little things really are. I give thanks to God for everything I can think of each day. Each time someone I know and love arrives safely to where they travel are those times I thank God as well.

I love walking and observing nature, animals, and even people. Walking is relaxing and invigorating, especially when we take in our surroundings. The sights, sounds, and smells during a walk can be pleasurable, so I walk to relax and enjoy the natural beauty wherever I go. I've spent hours walking on beaches, parks, fields, around ponds, and beside the oceans. Walking my dogs relaxed me. I always had a dog or two to walk and run with. Since the death of my last dog, I decided to wait until I was fully retired until I adopt another dog. How much I miss having dogs! Pets are precious creations that deserve our time and love as they unconditionally give their love to us. Having a dog or two was one of the best reasons I would run home after a workday since I became an empty nester.

I have an extravert personality, and I love socializing. I will smile and say hi to people that I walk by or while I am standing in line at the market. I don't care if people respond back to me. I don't take it personal. I'm going to be friendly anyway. A smile or gesture of friendship is positive, and it benefits all who give and receive it. Your smile or a polite gesture may be the only one that someone else receives. It feels good to me and may benefit someone else as well. Forging new friendships or acquaintances is fun and fulfilling for me. I have acquainted myself with many nice people in the community that I moved to. I'm involved with community and civic activities as I continue my relationships with my best friends and family.

Having a church to visit or being a member of one is a benefit in countless ways. Most churches lend support, friendship, and have activities. I have explored several churches where I now reside. I attended a church where I used to live that I do miss. I pray. I talk with God throughout my day everywhere I go. I chose to develop and grow a personal relationship with Jesus as I mentioned earlier in these writings. My life is better, more fulfilled, and joyful even when there are difficult times or days. God is my rock. I choose to grow in relationship with Him. At times I will remind myself of God's promise that I am loved by Him. It helps increase my faith and also adds a boost of positive reinforcement and strength.

I like fun, and I want to laugh more often. I actually have a sense of humor, but these writing are of serious nature, so that part of my personality did not get expressed much. I love being humorous. I could be spontaneous and sarcastically silly. It is part of who I am. I miss the days that humor was more acceptable and sought after. Though some of this has changed, I am not going to give up humor. When I do watch television, I view comedy shows and the older television shows that were simply made and had simple humor. So be silly more often and laugh, whether it is with others or just by yourself. I won't get offended.

I love to sing worship songs, whether they are classical or contemporary. I sing along with songs that stir up great memories and good feelings. Put on the golden oldies, Motown, classic rock, an occasional musical, or opera. I like all music. I played piano and clarinet in my middle and high-school years and was fortunate that three of my daughters chose to play a couple of musical instruments as well. My son developed other interests, but he is a good listener when my daughters would play in the school band. One of my daughters composed many musical pieces on the piano. A piano in our house is still a staple in my daughters' homes. Now some of my grandchildren are learning musical instruments. It is a delight observing their interests in music, as well as their school studies and other activities.

I'm grateful to be semiretired because I now have time to attend my grandchildren's activities and spend more quality time with them. My ten grandchildren are a large part of my happiest times, the reason life is even better than I could imagine. Grateful am I, and I give thanks often for the blessings of having children and grandchildren. I am grateful for the love they show me, and I love them with all my heart and soul. The little grands sometimes dance to some fun music I find for them, and I jump up and dance with them. I love to run around and dance with these kids. They are so funny, and it's a great way for everyone to burn up some energy. In my younger years, we danced almost every weekend year-round in the Wildwoods where I lived. I enjoyed those times that many of us went out to dance, you don't find much of that these days. Now, if there is a good song being played, and I am home alone, I dance in my home by myself. It stirs up good feelings, good memories, and it's great exercise as well. So sing and dance away, be joyous, and don't care who is watching or listening to you. I am free to be me. You are free to be you as long as it is all in a good way.

Chapter 16

Thank You

A big blessed thank-you to *all* who serve because their heart directs them to do so. I think of you, acknowledge you, and pray for you. Blessings to you who serve and are selfless, work hard, giving your all because you care. You may not get the paycheck you deserve for the work you do, but you give of you heart. What would we do without you? Many times you don't get a thank-you, instead you may get unwarranted criticism, excessive workloads, unsafe conditions, upper management that can be unrealistic and ungrateful, or the unreasonable demands legislated by government. God knows your heart. He values who you are, and you will reap what you sow. Words cannot describe the gratitude you deserve. I want to acknowledge the medical personnel first since my writings are focused on our jobs. I realize it would be impossible to list all who serve in every field known to humanity. For those who serve silently, discreetly, who are protecting citizens, rescuing people, and even animals, for those of you who are assisting or directly involved for the greater good, those who are volunteers—you are valued and treasured. We can't thank you enough.

Respiratory therapists: At this writing, I have twenty-five years working in hospitals, and two years in nursing facilities. The work we do is more than what is described on a job description. The number of respiratory therapists compared to the amount of work we do is disproportionate. In a community hospital, there may be perhaps two to three therapists in a shift. We work scheduled tasks, and we are running to every call, whether it is by phone, overhead announcements, or someone yelling for help. Calls for help and emergencies happen in any place any time in every part of the hospital. We drop what we are doing and run to where we are needed. We work in circumstances that have risks and dangers that affect us physically and emotionally. We are first responders as well as scheduled therapists in emergency, acute, and long-term care. The adrenaline that can flow through your body because we respond and run can lead to unhealthy body and mind. Our minds keep thinking of the next step or the next priority while we are completing the task at hand. We keep moving along from task to task, hoping not to make mistakes in the midst of many emergent situations. I have the privilege to work with some of the most dedicated respiratory therapists who have been key team players and caring colleagues. I won't forget you, and many of you are still in my life. Thank you.

Nurses RN and LPN, valued colleagues that are first in line with their patients' care: Your patients immensely rely on you for everything. You are their voice, the communicator between physicians, ancillary, patients' families, and others. I have the privilege to work with some of the best nurses. You are practitioners that made my shift a better one. Words cannot describe what you do in your job and the risks that are involved. Thank you.

Nurse aides: You have a job that is physically demanding, more than anyone can describe. The risks of injuries and disease are the same for you as it is for us. Your patients depend on you, look forward to seeing you. You are valued. Thank you.

Physicians: You are the ultimate decision-maker, prescriber, and the responsibilities fall heavily on you. You consult and take care of huge workloads of patients while adhering to rules and regulations and making tough decisions. Some of us realize that you are human and are not a computer with all the answers. Your quick thinking and skills cannot be described in words. Some people have unrealistic expectations of physicians; after all, physicians don't proclaim to be God. I've worked with some of the most dedicated and tireless doctors during my workdays. Most physicians do not make the salary that some may think, and many physicians are paid and bound by the hospitals that they work in. Knowing that most of the CEOs and some upper management earn more money than a physician earns is still unfathomable. Thank you.

Physician assistants and nurse practitioners: You are a right hand. I respect your positions. You put in countless hours in this very responsible and needed job. Thank you.

Physical therapists, occupational therapists, diagnostic personnel, the job is demanding. Responsibilities are endless. We see your hard work. Thank you.

Patient transporters: You endlessly and safely assist patients. Your job is physically demanding. I appreciate the teamwork I had with you to transport and assist our patients. Thank you.

Medical assistants of any kind, the cleanup crew, including housekeepers, especially those who work in the ER: Your job is physically and constantly ongoing and demanding. You are valued. Thank you.

US military—past, present, and future *heroes*: You don't get the praise you deserve, choosing to volunteer to protect our country. You deserve highest respect because you bravely consented to the demands that are imposed on you. Thank you.

Police, firefighters, EMT, paramedics, border patrol, rescuers of all kinds: You are the first responders who jump into dangerous, unknown situations. Highest respect to all of you. I can't imagine how life would be without you. Thank you.

Human rescuers, animal rescuers: You roll with your hearts dedicated to your cause. Thank you.

Unknown security personnel of all kinds, serving humanity: We don't see you; we don't know your job. Your brave service is helping us have freedom. Thank you.

Caretakers, dedicated parents, volunteers: You're valued more than you know, especially by those who are the most vulnerable. You are led by your hearts and conviction. Thank you.

> Therefore encourage one another and build up one another, just as you also are doing. (1 Thessalonians 5:11)

> For you are called to freedom, brethren; only do not turn your freedom into an opportunity for the flesh, but through love serve one another. (Galatians 5:13)

> Commit your works to the Lord and your plans will be established. (Proverbs 16:3)

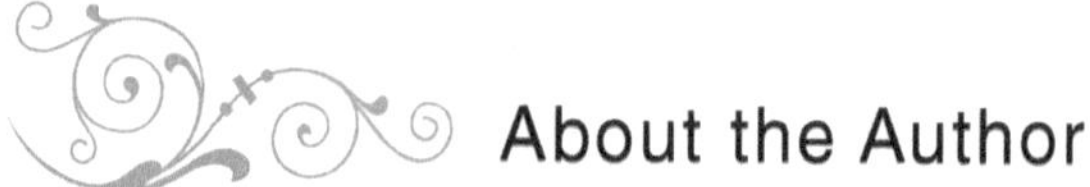

About the Author

Gina Sanguinetti is a registered respiratory therapist for twenty-seven years and is still currently working in this job. She was working full-time in the hospital systems in New Jersey for twenty-five years. After moving from her roots of sixty-two years from North Wildwood, New Jersey, she is currently working as needed in a nursing and rehab in Lancaster, Pennsylvania, where she now resides. She participates in local civic activities and is currently serving as local committee person. She enjoys being active, exercise workouts, and continues to strive for a lifestyle of good health and fitness. She is a proud mom of four adult children and adores her ten beautiful grandchildren.